3x28

A Case Study of
The Dead Internet Theory

Sam A. Casivio

THE EVOLUTION OF THE INTERNET: FROM HUMAN-CENTERED INTERACTION TO THE PRESENT FORM

The internet, since its inception, has undergone a profound transformation. What began as a tool for connecting a small group of academic and government researchers has grown into a vast digital ecosystem that impacts nearly every aspect of modern life. The internet's evolution has been shaped by technological advancements, the increasing role of corporations, and changing user behaviors. Today, we see an internet that is largely influenced by algorithms, artificial intelligence, and a shift towards commercialism, but it still retains aspects of human-centered interaction that defined its early years. This essay explores the evolution of the internet, highlighting the transition from its early stages of human-centered interaction to its present form.

The Early Internet: Human-Centered Interaction

The origins of the internet date back to the late 1960s with the development of ARPANET (Advanced Research Projects Agency Network), a project funded by the U.S. Department of Defense. Originally designed to allow researchers to share information and communicate over long distances, the early internet was a platform centered on human-to-human communication. Early users were primarily academics and government officials who connected to share research and ideas. The internet was built on the ethos of collaboration and open access to knowledge.

In the 1990s, the internet became more accessible to the general public with the advent of the World Wide Web, developed by Tim Berners-Lee. The introduction of web browsers like Netscape and Internet Explorer allowed users to access websites with ease. The internet was still highly human-centered during this time, with personal websites, forums, and blogs flourishing as platforms for individuals to share their thoughts and creations. Communities of like-minded individuals could connect through message boards and online chat rooms, enabling a sense of virtual camaraderie. The early internet was primarily a space for self-expression, exploration, and interaction between individuals who were united by common interests, regardless of physical location.

During this period, content was largely user-generated, and the internet was seen as a decentralized space where individuals could communicate and create freely. Websites like GeoCities and Angelfire allowed people to build their own websites, and platforms like AOL Instant Messenger and early versions of Yahoo! facilitated direct, real-time communication. Search engines like AltaVista and Ask Jeeves were primitive tools that helped users navigate this vast digital landscape, but the focus remained on facilitating human-driven interactions.

The Rise of Social Media and Commercialization

The early 2000s marked a turning point in the evolution of the internet. As broadband connections became more widespread, the internet's capacity for multimedia content, such as images and video, grew exponentially. In 2004, the launch of Facebook signified a major shift towards social media, and platforms like MySpace and Friendster set the stage for the explosion of online social networks. These platforms facilitated deeper connections between users, enabling them to share photos, statuses, and life updates, marking a new era of personalized interaction.

The rise of social media also brought about a commercialization of the internet. As online engagement grew, businesses recognized the potential of the internet for marketing and advertising. This led to the dominance of platforms like Facebook, Google, and later Instagram, which began to shape the content that users saw based on algorithms designed to maximize user engagement. These algorithms, designed to keep users scrolling, began to prioritize content that was most likely to elicit clicks, shares, or likes, which often meant sensationalist or emotionally charged content. While this increased engagement, it also shifted the internet away from its roots of organic, user-generated content to a space dominated by corporate interests and algorithmic manipulation.

At the same time, the internet's ability to connect people across the globe expanded. Platforms like YouTube (founded in 2005) and Twitter (founded in 2006) allowed for real-time sharing of ideas and news, bringing a global dimension to human-centered interaction. People could now broadcast their thoughts to the world with the click of a button, creating new opportunities for social activism, political discourse, and cultural exchange. However, as these platforms grew, they became more centralized, with a few powerful companies controlling the majority of the digital experience. This era saw the rise of influencer culture, with individuals leveraging social media to build massive followings, often leading to a shift in internet interactions from purely communal to commercially driven.

The Current Internet: Algorithmic Control and AI Integration

Today, the internet is vastly different from the early days of human-centered interaction. The internet of the present is dominated by powerful corporations, highly personalized algorithms, and artificial intelligence (AI). Platforms like Google, Facebook, YouTube, and Amazon not only provide services but also curate content through complex algorithms that determine what users see, read, and engage with. These algorithms rely on data, tracking user behavior to offer a tailored experience that maximizes engagement and profits. As a result, much of the internet has become a space where human interaction is often mediated by machines—AI-driven content curation, automated chatbots, and even deepfake technology have become more prevalent.

Social media platforms are no longer just spaces for individuals to connect with friends and family. Instead, they have evolved into ecosystems that encourage passive consumption of content through endless scrolling and algorithm-driven feeds. The rise of TikTok, for instance, has shown how short-form, algorithmically tailored video content has become a dominant mode of interaction. Here, AI plays a significant role in determining which videos go viral based on a user's past interactions, creating a cycle where content is served based on past preferences, rather than fostering new or diverse interactions.

Furthermore, the proliferation of e-commerce platforms, streaming services, and digital advertising has made the internet a highly commercialized space. Companies now track user behavior across multiple devices and platforms, using data to predict and influence purchasing decisions, while also shaping the way content is presented to users. As a result, human-centered interaction has become less organic and more transactional. Users are often treated as data points that can be analyzed and targeted for advertising, rather than as active participants in an open, decentralized digital world.

Considerations

The internet has evolved from a human-centered space of open communication and creativity to a complex digital landscape that is heavily influenced by algorithms, artificial intelligence, and corporate interests. In its early years, the internet was a decentralized, user-driven platform where individuals could freely express themselves, share ideas, and connect with others. Today, however, it has become a commercialized and algorithmically curated space, where user behavior is tracked, analyzed, and monetized by large tech companies. Despite these changes, the internet remains a powerful tool for human connection, but the balance between user-generated content and machine-driven interaction continues to shift. As the internet continues to evolve, it will be important to navigate the challenges of algorithmic control and commercialization while striving to preserve the authentic, human-centered qualities that made the internet so transformative in its early days.

THE DEAD INTERNET THEORY: AN OVERVIEW

The "Dead Internet Theory" is a controversial and speculative conspiracy theory suggesting that much of the internet, as we know it, has been overtaken by artificial intelligence (AI), bots, and algorithmic content, rather than being an authentic space for human interaction and creativity. Proponents of the theory argue that the internet, once a thriving ecosystem of personal blogs, forums, and human-generated content, is now largely artificial and manipulated by unseen entities, corporations, and AI systems. This essay provides an overview of the Dead Internet Theory, its origins, the key ideas behind it, and the arguments both for and against it.

The Origin and Core Premise of the Dead Internet Theory

The Dead Internet Theory emerged from growing concerns about the increasing role of bots, algorithms, and AI in shaping the modern internet. It suggests that the internet's initial promise, where users could freely create and engage with one another, has been replaced with automated content and artificial interactions. According to proponents, much of what we see online today is either generated by AI systems or manipulated by bots in ways that obscure the genuine human voices that once populated the web.

One of the core assertions of the theory is that, over time, the percentage of real human interactions on the internet has sharply declined, while automated content, bots, and algorithmically generated posts have flooded social media, news websites, and search engines. The Dead Internet Theory claims that what we experience today is a "zombified" version of the internet, where engagement is driven not by individual expression but by an invisible, controlling network of artificial actors.

Key Concepts Behind the Dead Internet Theory

Several key ideas underlie the Dead Internet Theory, most of which focus on the ways that modern technologies, particularly artificial intelligence and automation, have reshaped the digital landscape.

1. *Rise of Bots and Automation*: One of the primary arguments in favor of the theory is the increasing prevalence of bots and automated systems on the internet. Bots are programs that can simulate human behavior, creating fake social media accounts, posting comments, and even generating news articles or product reviews. Proponents of the Dead Internet Theory argue that bots have become so numerous that real human interaction online is now a minority, with automated content and interactions dominating online spaces.

2. *Algorithmic Control*: Another critical aspect of the theory is the rise of algorithms that govern much of what we see online. Social media platforms, search engines, and even news websites now rely on complex algorithms to curate content and dictate user engagement. These algorithms prioritize content that maximizes engagement, often favoring sensationalism, clickbait, or artificial interactions. According to the theory, this has led to a homogenization of online content, with the diversity and creativity that characterized the early days of the internet now buried beneath algorithmically optimized content.

3. *AI-Generated Content*: The theory also suggests that AI-generated content, including text, images, and videos, is filling much of the space once occupied by human-generated material. With the advancement of machine learning models like OpenAI's GPT and image generators like DALL·E, the internet is seeing an explosion of AI-created material that mimics human creativity but often lacks depth, authenticity, or emotional resonance. Critics of this development argue that this content, while often indistinguishable from human-made content, undermines the genuine, organic nature of the internet.

4. *Corporate Influence and Censorship*: Another factor that the Dead Internet Theory addresses is the growing influence of large corporations and government entities on online content. With a few tech giants like Google, Meta (Facebook), and Amazon controlling much of the internet's infrastructure, critics argue that these companies prioritize their own financial interests over the free expression of individuals. This centralization has led to concerns about censorship, content manipulation, and surveillance, which proponents of the Dead Internet Theory believe contributes to the perception that the internet is no longer a place of open, organic human interaction.

Arguments Supporting the Dead Internet Theory

The Dead Internet Theory garners support from several concerns about the current state of the internet and its increasing reliance on AI, bots, and algorithmic control. Some of the primary arguments in favor of the theory include:

1. *Prevalence of Fake Accounts and Bots*: Studies and data have shown that a significant percentage of social media accounts, particularly on platforms like Twitter and Instagram, are either fake or automated. According to some estimates, bots account for up to 20% or more of Twitter accounts, and many of these bots are involved in amplifying political discourse, spreading misinformation, or manipulating public opinion.
2. *Decline of Organic Content*: Once thriving platforms like independent blogs, personal forums, and even comment sections on websites have largely given way to centralized platforms controlled by big tech companies. Many independent voices are being drowned out by algorithm-driven content that prioritizes sensationalism and engagement over quality or individuality.
3. *Artificial Content Overload*: With the rise of AI, much of the content online today—ranging from product reviews to news articles and even creative works like poems or artwork—is AI-generated. Some critics claim that this saturation of artificial content reduces the uniqueness and authenticity of the internet, making it feel more like a controlled and less human space.

Counterarguments to the Dead Internet Theory

While the Dead Internet Theory has gained traction among certain online communities, it is important to acknowledge that it has been widely criticized and is largely unsubstantiated by mainstream researchers. Some of the key counterarguments include:

1. *The Internet is Simply Evolving*: Many critics argue that the internet is not dead but simply evolving. Just as the

internet has changed in the past—from static webpages to dynamic social media platforms—today's internet is adapting to new technological advancements, including AI. This evolution, while sometimes unsettling, does not necessarily mean the internet is no longer authentic or human-centered.

2. *AI and Automation as Tools, Not Replacements*: Another counterargument is that AI and bots are simply tools that help enhance online experiences, not replace human interaction. For example, AI can assist in moderating content, improving user experience, and even generating creative ideas, but humans remain integral to the creation and consumption of content. Proponents of this view argue that while automation may change how content is created, it does not diminish the internet's overall human-driven nature.

3. *Real, Human-Centered Content Still Exists*: Despite the dominance of algorithms and AI, there are still vast, thriving communities on the internet where real human engagement occurs. Independent content creators, niche communities, and grassroots movements continue to flourish, suggesting that the internet has not been entirely overtaken by artificial content.

Considerations

The Dead Internet Theory offers a provocative lens through which to examine the current state of the internet and the role of automation, AI, and algorithms in shaping our online experiences. While the theory highlights valid concerns about the increasing influence of technology and corporate interests, it remains speculative and lacks strong empirical evidence to fully support its claims. As the internet continues to evolve, it will be important for users to remain critical of the forces shaping their digital environments, but also to recognize that human-driven content, creativity, and interaction still play a central role in the fabric of the online world. The challenge lies in ensuring that technology serves to enhance, rather than replace, the authentic human connections that have long been at the heart of the internet.

THE EARLY DAYS OF THE INTERNET: ORIGINS AND VIBRANT HUMAN ENGAGEMENT IN THE 1990S AND EARLY 2000S

The internet, as we know it today, has undergone significant transformations since its inception. In its early days, the internet was a dynamic space for personal expression, creativity, and human connection. From the late 1980s through the early 2000s, the internet was primarily a tool for human engagement, where individuals interacted with one another through forums, early social media, and personal websites. These formative years laid the foundation for the vast digital ecosystem we now navigate, but they also provided a more organic and human-centered experience than what we see today. This essay explores the internet's origins in the 1990s and early 2000s, highlighting how vibrant human engagement characterized this era, including the rise of forums, early social media platforms, and personal websites.

Origins of the Internet: The Birth of the World Wide Web (1990s)

The internet as we know it began to take shape in the late 1980s and early 1990s. However, it was in 1991 that the creation of the World Wide Web by British computer scientist Tim Berners-Lee revolutionized the way humans could access and share information. Before the web, networks like ARPANET had allowed researchers to communicate and share data, but the World Wide Web provided a more user-friendly, visual interface that anyone with access to a computer could navigate. This marked the beginning of a new era in which individuals could use the internet for far more than just academic or governmental purposes.

The early 1990s saw the creation of the first web browsers—Mosaic (released in 1993) and Netscape Navigator (released in 1994)—that allowed users to access and view websites. The invention of these browsers made the internet more accessible to the general public, and by the mid-1990s, the internet started to grow exponentially. During this period, the internet was still a largely uncharted frontier, and it was populated by early adopters—technically savvy individuals and communities interested in exploring what this new medium had to offer.

The digital ecosystem of the 1990s was built around the concept of human engagement. Users interacted with each other on new platforms designed for sharing ideas and building connections. The lack of centralization in the early internet encouraged innovation and creativity, with individuals creating their own corners of the web to express themselves.

The Rise of Forums and Online Communities

One of the defining features of the early internet was the development of forums and online communities. These spaces allowed users to connect over shared interests, exchange information, and form meaningful relationships with people across the globe. Forums, which were essentially bulletin board systems (BBS), served as virtual meeting places where individuals could post messages, start discussions, and respond to others' ideas. Websites like Usenet, which hosted thousands of newsgroups, and platforms like The WELL (The Whole Earth 'Lectronic Link) in the early 1990s, offered spaces for intellectual exchange and the democratization of ideas.

The discussions that took place on these early forums were often driven by specific interests or communities, ranging from hobbies like gaming or technology to more niche topics such as politics or philosophy. These forums allowed people to communicate freely and without many of the barriers that existed in physical spaces. A wide range of individuals, from experts in their fields to everyday users, participated in these digital dialogues. Some of these communities, like the *alt.* newsgroups and specialized hobbyist forums, remain important examples of how the early internet was a decentralized space where individuals could shape conversations.

Forums during this era were often text-heavy, lacking the visual appeal or interactivity we associate with modern websites. Nevertheless, they were rich in human interaction, with users offering advice, sharing experiences, and developing friendships. The focus was on creating valuable content and fostering conversations, and the sense of anonymity offered by the internet allowed for open and candid exchanges that might not have been possible in real life. This communal aspect of the early internet provided a foundation for the social nature of the digital world that would continue to grow in the coming decades.

Personal Websites and Early Social Media

Along with forums, personal websites were a cornerstone of early internet culture. In the mid-1990s, individuals began to create websites to express themselves, showcase their interests, or even to establish a presence online. These personal pages were often rudimentary, featuring text, images, and basic HTML formatting. Popular website builders like GeoCities (founded in 1994) allowed individuals to create websites with relative ease, even if they did not have advanced technical skills. People could now present their thoughts, art, music, and hobbies to a global audience.

The personal website era was also marked by a spirit of creativity and individuality. Users would often customize their web pages with colorful backgrounds, animated GIFs, guestbooks, and personal commentary. The internet in this period was characterized by an abundance of personal expression, as people built their digital identities on these custom sites. Many early internet users maintained personal blogs or journals on their pages, offering a glimpse into their daily lives and thoughts, long before platforms like WordPress or Tumblr popularized blogging.

While personal websites were initially independent and decentralized, the late 1990s saw the first forms of centralized social media platforms beginning to emerge. Early examples of social networking sites included Six Degrees (founded in 1997) and Friendster (launched in 2002), which allowed users to create profiles, connect with friends, and share content. Though these early social media platforms were far simpler than what would come later with Facebook and Twitter, they marked the first steps toward building online identities and social networks in a more structured format.

These platforms were designed to enhance human connections and, in many ways, replicated the sense of community that forums and personal websites had fostered. However, social media platforms quickly began to evolve beyond simple human connection, leading to the eventual rise of more commercialized and algorithmically driven platforms in the following decades.

Vibrant Human Engagement and the Growth of the Internet

During the late 1990s and early 2000s, the internet was a space largely defined by human engagement. There was a sense of exploration and discovery as people from all over the world connected in ways that were previously impossible. The internet felt like a virtual extension of real-world social networks, where individuals could contribute, create, and interact on their own terms.

Although the infrastructure of the internet was still primitive by today's standards, there was a tangible sense of enthusiasm for the possibilities it offered. The internet was still a relatively new phenomenon, and its social, cultural, and economic potential was only beginning to be recognized. From creative forums to the rise of early social media platforms and personal websites, users were driving the culture and content of the digital landscape.

As the internet expanded in the early 2000s, commercial interests began to emerge. Companies recognized the internet's potential for marketing, advertising, and e-commerce. Yet, despite this growing commercialization, the early 2000s were still a time when much of the content and engagement online was driven by individuals—people sharing their thoughts, connecting with others, and creating digital spaces that reflected their identities and interests.

Considerations

The early days of the internet, from the 1990s to the early 2000s, were marked by vibrant human engagement. It was a period where individuals had the freedom to create, connect, and express themselves in ways that were previously impossible. Online forums, personal websites, and early social media platforms all played a crucial role in shaping the internet into a space for organic, user-generated content. The internet's decentralized, human-centered nature during this time laid the foundation for the digital world we live in today, providing a glimpse of a more open and interactive digital ecosystem that allowed people to communicate and create freely. As the internet has evolved, the sense of individual expression and community engagement from its early days remains an essential part of its legacy.

THE GROWTH OF SOCIAL MEDIA AND COMMERCIALISM: THE EVOLUTION OF PLATFORMS LIKE FACEBOOK, TWITTER, AND INSTAGRAM

The rise of social media has dramatically reshaped the digital landscape over the past two decades. What started as simple communication tools for connecting with friends and sharing personal updates has evolved into powerful platforms for business, marketing, politics, and social movements. Social media platforms like Facebook, Twitter, and Instagram have transformed from being primarily focused on human interaction to becoming hubs of commercialization, driven by advertising revenue and data analytics. This essay explores the growth of social media, its increasing commercialization, and how platforms like Facebook, Twitter, and Instagram have evolved to dominate the digital world.

The Early Days of Social Media: A Focus on Connection and Communication

In the early 2000s, the internet was a space for individuals to connect, share, and communicate with others around the world. Early social media platforms like Six Degrees (1997), Friendster (2002), and MySpace (2003) were built on the idea of fostering relationships, primarily by allowing users to create profiles and connect with friends. These platforms were relatively simple, offering basic social networking features such as the ability to post personal information, upload photos, and message other users.

However, it was the launch of Facebook in 2004 that marked the beginning of a new era in social media. Facebook initially focused on connecting college students but quickly expanded its user base to the general public. Its user-friendly interface, features like status updates, and focus on connecting with real friends made it the most popular social network of the early 2000s. Facebook's success sparked a wave of innovation in social media, with platforms like Twitter and Instagram emerging shortly after, each contributing new ways for individuals to interact online.

Twitter, founded in 2006, allowed users to post short, 140-character updates known as "tweets," creating a space for real-time conversations and information sharing. The simplicity of Twitter's design encouraged its rapid adoption by a wide range of users, from ordinary people to celebrities, journalists, and public figures. The platform's focus on brevity, immediacy, and trending topics made it particularly popular during breaking news events and political discussions.

Instagram, launched in 2010, added a visual element to the social media landscape. With its focus on sharing photos and videos, Instagram quickly gained popularity, particularly among younger audiences. Its visually-driven platform encouraged users to share personal moments, create aesthetically pleasing content, and follow influencers—users with large followings who could promote brands, products, or lifestyles. Instagram's emphasis on visual storytelling allowed it to grow rapidly and became one of the most influential platforms in the social media ecosystem.

In the early days of social media, the primary focus of these platforms was on human engagement. They were spaces for users to connect with friends, share life updates, and engage with content that was interesting or entertaining. The commercial potential of these platforms was not yet fully realized, as the platforms were more focused on building user bases and increasing engagement.

The Shift Towards Commercialism: Monetizing Social Media

As social media platforms grew in popularity, the commercial potential of these networks became apparent. Platforms like Facebook, Twitter, and Instagram attracted millions, then billions, of active users. This massive audience made them highly attractive to businesses looking to advertise their products or services. The shift toward commercialization began in earnest around the mid-2000s as these platforms introduced advertising models designed to monetize user engagement.

Facebook led the way in monetizing social media with its advertising model. In 2007, Facebook introduced its "Facebook Ads" program, which allowed businesses to create targeted ads based on user data, such as age, location, interests, and online behavior. This targeted advertising approach, powered by Facebook's vast trove of user data, proved to be highly effective and was soon adopted by other platforms. As a result, advertising revenue became a significant driver of these platforms' growth and success. By offering businesses the ability to reach specific demographics with personalized content, Facebook set the stage for social media to become a key component of modern marketing strategies.

Twitter followed a similar path by introducing Promoted Tweets in 2010, allowing businesses to pay for their tweets to appear in the feeds of users who might not follow their accounts. The introduction of sponsored content marked a shift in Twitter's focus from being a space for public discourse to being a platform for advertisers to target users. Twitter's reliance on paid advertising grew in subsequent years, particularly as it struggled to generate revenue in other areas.

Instagram, too, capitalized on its popularity with users, particularly among younger demographics. Acquired by

Facebook in 2012, Instagram integrated advertising into its feed and stories. The visual nature of Instagram made it an ideal platform for businesses to promote products through eye-catching images and video. Influencer marketing also became a significant trend on Instagram, with users leveraging their large followings to partner with brands and create sponsored content. Instagram's algorithmic feed, which prioritizes posts based on user engagement, further encouraged businesses to tailor their content for maximum visibility.

As these platforms grew more commercial, the user experience also began to change. What was once an open space for free and organic communication became increasingly influenced by paid content, advertisements, and algorithm-driven feeds. Social media users now found their experiences shaped by algorithms designed to maximize engagement, which often meant that sensational, emotionally charged, or controversial content was more likely to be seen. The result was a shift from user-driven content creation to platform-driven content curation, where businesses, brands, and influencers played an increasingly prominent role.

The Evolution of Facebook, Twitter, and Instagram: Dominating the Digital Landscape

Today, Facebook, Twitter, and Instagram are dominant forces in the digital landscape, shaping everything from online communication to marketing, entertainment, and politics. These platforms have evolved beyond simple tools for social interaction into comprehensive ecosystems that encompass advertising, e-commerce, and content creation.

Facebook, for instance, has grown into a vast platform that serves as a hub for everything from news consumption and political discourse to gaming and e-commerce. With more than

2.8 billion monthly active users, Facebook has become a central part of many people's daily lives. The company has integrated shopping features, allowing businesses to set up storefronts within the platform, and has further embraced video content with features like Facebook Live and Watch. As Facebook has become more commercial, its focus on engagement through targeted advertising has driven its revenue model, with businesses paying for access to highly specific user groups.

Twitter, although it has faced challenges in terms of user growth and profitability, remains an influential platform in shaping real-time news and public discourse. Twitter has become a vital tool for journalists, politicians, celebrities, and ordinary citizens to comment on current events and express opinions. Despite its role in global discussions, Twitter has faced criticism for its algorithmic bias and its handling of harassment and misinformation. Still, it continues to dominate conversations in the digital world, particularly in the realm of politics and activism.

Instagram, now one of the most popular social media platforms, has revolutionized marketing with its visual-first approach. With over 1.4 billion monthly active users, Instagram has become a major platform for influencer marketing, where individuals leverage their large followings to promote products, services, and lifestyles. Instagram's Stories feature, which allows users to post temporary content, has become a vital part of its engagement strategy, with brands using it to promote limited-time offers or behind-the-scenes content. The introduction of Instagram Shopping and the ability to make purchases directly through the platform further solidified its position as a commercial powerhouse in the digital landscape.

These platforms have transformed social media from a space for individual interaction to a commercialized, algorithm-driven environment. The introduction of targeted advertising, influencer marketing, and e-commerce has led to a new economy built on user engagement and data. As a result, businesses, brands, and influencers now play a major role in shaping the content that circulates on these platforms, which has fundamentally altered the way people interact online.

Considerations

The growth of social media and its increasing commercialization have radically transformed the digital landscape. Platforms like Facebook, Twitter, and Instagram have evolved from simple tools for human connection into powerful commercial ecosystems driven by targeted advertising, influencer marketing, and data analytics. These platforms now dominate the digital world, shaping everything from how we communicate to how we consume information and products. While the early days of social media were characterized by organic, user-driven engagement, today's social media is a complex interplay of user interaction and business interests. As these platforms continue to evolve, the challenge will be finding a balance between commercialization and maintaining spaces for authentic human engagement.

THE RISE OF AUTOMATED SYSTEMS: HOW BOTS ARE FILLING THE INTERNET WITH NON-HUMAN CONTENT

The internet has become an integral part of everyday life, serving as a source of communication, information, entertainment, and commerce. As the digital landscape continues to evolve, a significant and often overlooked development is the increasing use of automated systems, commonly known as bots, which are filling the internet with non-human content. These bots are transforming the ways in which information is disseminated, opinions are expressed, and interactions take place. From social media platforms to news websites and comment sections, bots are shaping the online experience, often without users being fully aware of their presence. This essay explores the growing role of bots in the digital world, examining how they function and providing examples of their increasing presence on social media, news websites, and comment sections.

What Are Bots? Understanding the Rise of Automated Systems

At their core, bots are automated programs designed to perform specific tasks, typically mimicking human behavior, but at a much faster pace and scale. Bots can execute simple actions, such as sending messages or clicking links, or they can be more sophisticated, generating human-like text, images, or videos. They are typically powered by artificial intelligence (AI) and machine learning algorithms that enable them to perform complex tasks like analyzing large sets of data or interacting with humans in real-time.

Bots have become an essential part of the digital ecosystem, especially as the demand for content creation, customer service, and data analysis has grown. However, the presence of bots is not always apparent, and their increasing ability to blend seamlessly into online environments raises concerns about authenticity, misinformation, and the overall integrity of the internet. While some bots serve legitimate functions, such as providing customer support or streamlining data collection, others contribute to the spread of spam, fake news, and even influence public opinion.

Bots on Social Media: Amplifying Voices and Spreading Misinformation

One of the most visible areas where bots are making their mark is on social media platforms. Bots are widely used to amplify messages, spread political propaganda, and manipulate public opinion. They can generate fake likes, retweets, and shares, creating the illusion of popularity or consensus around certain topics or individuals. A prime example of this is the use of bots in political campaigns, where they can influence elections by amplifying particular viewpoints or flooding social media feeds with misleading or divisive content.

For example, during the 2016 U.S. presidential election, it was widely reported that Russian state-sponsored bots were active on platforms like Twitter and Facebook, spreading disinformation and attempting to sway voter sentiment. These bots used algorithms to create fake accounts, post politically charged content, and even interact with human users to make their influence appear more legitimate. The use of bots to push partisan agendas has become a common feature of modern political discourse, with bots used to manipulate public sentiment during elections around the world.

Bots are also employed by corporations and marketers to promote products or services through automated posts and comments. For instance, "like bots" are used to artificially inflate the popularity of content, making posts appear more widely shared or liked than they truly are. This can mislead consumers into thinking a product or idea is more popular or reputable than it actually is. Influencer marketing has further exacerbated this trend, with bots sometimes used to boost the follower counts of influencers, creating a false sense of authority or influence. This highlights a key issue with bots: their ability to manipulate perception and create a distorted reality on social media.

The role of bots in social media is also evident in the proliferation of "hate bots" and "troll bots." These automated systems are designed to generate harmful, offensive, or divisive content in an effort to polarize public opinion and disrupt online conversations. These bots often mimic human interaction, engaging with other users in ways that create outrage or provoke arguments. As a result, these bots contribute to the deterioration of online discourse, making it more toxic and less productive.

Bots on News Websites: Generating Content and Spreading Fake News

In addition to social media, bots are increasingly being used on news websites to automate the process of content creation and distribution. While automated news generation can serve legitimate purposes, such as quickly reporting on sports scores or stock market changes, it can also be used to create and spread fake news.

Bots on news websites can automatically generate articles based on data feeds or algorithms. These systems can write articles about breaking news events by pulling information from a variety of sources and combining it into a coherent narrative. This kind of automation is common in areas such as financial reporting or weather updates, where the structure of the story is predictable and factual. However, the same technology can be manipulated to produce misleading or false information, particularly in cases where bots are used to write sensationalized stories designed to attract attention and generate traffic.

A particularly concerning example of bot-driven content is the proliferation of fake news. During events like elections or natural disasters, bots can flood news websites with fake stories, generating clicks and spreading misinformation. Bots may also write "clickbait" headlines or fake reviews, which can deceive readers and lead them to consume false or biased information. These stories are often shared through social media platforms, further amplifying their reach and making it more difficult for users to distinguish between credible news sources and fabricated content.

A notable instance of this occurred during the 2016 U.S. presidential election, when bots were used to spread fabricated stories and false headlines, targeting certain demographic groups with tailored disinformation. These bots were able to produce large volumes of content quickly, creating a sense of urgency and legitimacy around false narratives. As bots continue to evolve, their ability to generate increasingly sophisticated fake news raises significant concerns about the integrity of information online.

Bots in Comment Sections: Disrupting Conversations and Amplifying Bias

Comment sections on news websites, blogs, and social media platforms are another area where bots have gained prominence. Bots are often used to post comments that either spam the platform with irrelevant or promotional content, or they are strategically deployed to influence discussions. In some cases, bots are programmed to post comments that reflect a particular agenda, amplify specific viewpoints, or disrupt conversations by flooding comment sections with repetitive or inflammatory content.

For instance, bots may be used to flood a comment section with positive feedback about a particular product, company, or political figure, creating a false sense of public approval. This type of manipulation, known as "astroturfing," is a form of fake grassroots campaigning that can make a certain topic or viewpoint appear more popular than it really is. On the other hand, bots can also be used to attack or harass individuals in comment sections, creating a hostile online environment and silencing dissenting opinions.

The rise of "troll bots" is another example of how bots are shaping online interactions. These bots are programmed to post offensive, inflammatory, or provocative comments in order to provoke emotional responses and escalate conflicts. Troll bots can create an environment of hostility and division, leading to the breakdown of productive discussions and the spread of negativity online.

Bots in comment sections can also be used to promote conspiracy theories or spread misinformation. They can post links to fake websites or blogs, driving traffic to disreputable sources and further contributing to the spread of false narratives. This undermines the credibility of legitimate discussions and makes it harder for users to find reliable information.

Considerations

As automated systems (bots) increasingly fill the internet with non-human content, they are reshaping the way we interact with digital platforms. Bots have become powerful tools for manipulating social media, generating fake news, and disrupting online conversations. While bots can offer valuable functions, such as automating tasks and providing customer service, their use in spreading misinformation, amplifying bias, and distorting public opinion raises serious concerns about the integrity of the internet.

To address these challenges, there is a growing need for regulation and oversight to limit the harmful effects of bots. Social media platforms and news organizations must develop stronger measures to detect and prevent the use of bots for malicious purposes. Additionally, users must become more aware of the presence of bots and their potential to influence online interactions. Only by taking these steps can we ensure that the internet remains a space for authentic human engagement and information exchange.

THE IMPACT OF AI-GENERATED CONTENT: DEEPFAKE VIDEOS, AI-WRITTEN ARTICLES, AND AUTOMATED CONVERSATIONS IN CUSTOMER SERVICE

Artificial Intelligence (AI) has rapidly advanced in recent years, bringing profound changes to various industries and transforming the way humans interact with technology. One of the most significant developments has been the creation of AI-generated content, which includes deepfake videos, AI-written articles, and automated customer service conversations. While these technologies hold immense potential, they also raise critical concerns regarding their ethical implications, security risks, and impact on human labor. This essay explores the impact of AI-generated content, focusing on deepfake videos, AI-written articles, and automated customer service conversations, while examining the benefits and challenges posed by these innovations.

Deepfake Videos: Manipulation and Misinformation

Deepfakes are AI-generated videos or images that manipulate real footage, creating realistic but entirely fabricated content. They use sophisticated machine learning techniques, particularly Generative Adversarial Networks (GANs), to produce videos where a person's likeness, voice, or even actions can be altered to portray them saying or doing things they never actually did. Deepfakes have gained significant attention due to their potential to deceive audiences and their use in spreading misinformation.

One of the most alarming consequences of deepfake technology is its ability to create convincing fake videos of public figures, celebrities, or even private individuals, which can be used to manipulate public opinion, defame people, or spread political propaganda. For example, deepfake videos have been used to create fake political speeches or news reports, making it appear as though a political leader made statements that could damage their reputation or influence elections. In 2018, a deepfake video of former U.S. President Barack Obama was created by the nonprofit organization Buzzfeed in collaboration with actor Jordan Peele to raise awareness about the potential dangers of the technology. The video showed Obama delivering a speech he had never made, demonstrating how easily deepfakes could be used to deceive viewers.

The growing prevalence of deepfake content has raised concerns about the erosion of trust in media and the potential for widespread misinformation. As AI technology improves, it becomes increasingly difficult for viewers to distinguish between real and fake content. This creates significant challenges for verifying the authenticity of information online and maintaining the credibility of traditional media outlets. Additionally, deepfakes can be used for malicious purposes, such as blackmail, defamation, or harassment, where fabricated videos are created to discredit individuals or institutions. The legal and ethical questions surrounding deepfakes, such as the rights of individuals whose likenesses are misused, remain unresolved and present a challenge for policymakers.

However, deepfake technology is not only used for nefarious purposes. It also has potential in creative fields, such as film production, where filmmakers can digitally recreate actors or generate realistic special effects. While these uses may offer innovative opportunities, the overall impact of deepfake technology on society is complicated by the potential for misuse.

AI-Written Articles: Automation in Journalism and Content Creation

AI-written articles are another form of AI-generated content that is increasingly being used across various sectors, particularly in journalism, marketing, and content creation. Tools like OpenAI's GPT-3 and similar language models are capable of generating coherent and contextually relevant text based on a given prompt, enabling machines to write articles, blog posts, product descriptions, and even creative content like poetry or stories. These AI systems are trained on vast amounts of data and use algorithms to predict and generate text, making them a powerful tool for automating content production.

The use of AI to write articles has both advantages and disadvantages. On the positive side, AI can dramatically increase the efficiency of content production. News outlets, for example, use AI to write basic reports on topics like stock market updates, sports scores, and weather forecasts. This allows journalists to focus on more complex, investigative work. Additionally, AI-generated content can be tailored to target specific keywords and optimize search engine rankings, helping businesses improve their online visibility.

However, the rise of AI-written articles has raised concerns about the quality and accuracy of content. AI-generated content is based on patterns found in the data it has been trained on, but it may lack the nuance, critical thinking, and creativity that human writers bring to the table. This can lead to the production of repetitive, shallow, or inaccurate content that lacks depth or originality. In journalism, the reliance on AI-generated articles can compromise the integrity of news reporting, particularly if it leads to the automation of sensationalist or biased content. There is also the risk that AI-written articles could be used to spread misinformation or propaganda, as AI systems can easily generate articles that appear legitimate but are factually incorrect or misleading.

Moreover, the rise of AI in content creation raises important ethical issues regarding authorship and accountability. If an AI writes an article that contains false information or defamatory statements, who is responsible for the consequences? Should the creators of the AI be held accountable, or should the responsibility fall to the platform that published the content? These are questions that will need to be addressed as AI becomes more integrated into the content creation process.

Automated Conversations in Customer Service: Efficiency and Impersonalization

AI-powered chatbots and virtual assistants have revolutionized customer service by automating interactions between businesses and customers. These systems, often powered by natural language processing (NLP) algorithms, are capable of understanding customer inquiries and providing automated responses in real time. Many companies now use chatbots to handle a variety of customer service tasks, from answering frequently asked questions to processing transactions and troubleshooting technical issues.

The use of AI in customer service offers significant benefits, particularly in terms of efficiency and cost savings. Chatbots are available 24/7, meaning customers can receive immediate assistance regardless of time or location. They can handle routine inquiries quickly and accurately, freeing up human agents to focus on more complex or specialized tasks. This can result in shorter wait times for customers and improved customer satisfaction. Additionally, AI-driven systems can process large volumes of data, allowing companies to analyze customer interactions and improve their services over time.

However, the increasing reliance on automated conversations also brings challenges. One of the primary concerns is the lack of human empathy and emotional intelligence in AI-powered interactions. While chatbots can provide factual information and respond to basic queries, they often struggle to handle complex or sensitive issues that require a nuanced, empathetic response. This can lead to frustration for customers who feel that their concerns are not being fully addressed by an impersonal system. In some cases, AI systems can even misunderstand customer inquiries, leading to incorrect or unsatisfactory responses.

Additionally, the automation of customer service through AI raises questions about the future of human labor. As chatbots and virtual assistants become more advanced, there is the potential for job displacement, particularly for customer service agents who handle routine inquiries. This could lead to a shift in the workforce, with fewer human jobs available in areas traditionally dominated by customer support roles.

Balancing Innovation and Responsibility

AI-generated content, including deepfake videos, AI-written articles, and automated conversations in customer service, has the potential to transform industries and improve efficiency. These technologies can enhance creativity, automate routine tasks, and provide more personalized services. However, they also present significant challenges, including the spread of misinformation, the erosion of trust, and the potential for job displacement. The increasing use of AI-generated content requires careful consideration of ethical, legal, and social implications. As AI continues to advance, it will be crucial for policymakers, businesses, and society as a whole to find a balance between embracing innovation and ensuring that these technologies are used responsibly and ethically. Only by doing so can we harness the benefits of AI while mitigating its potential risks.

THE DEAD INTERNET THEORY: THE DECLINE OF ORGANIC CONTENT AND THE RISE OF AI-GENERATED MATERIAL

The Dead Internet Theory, a somewhat fringe and conspiratorial concept, posits that the internet as we once knew it — vibrant, filled with real human interactions and content — has largely died out. According to proponents of the theory, the internet is now being dominated by artificial intelligence (AI) systems and automated bots that generate content and interactions that mimic human behavior but are fundamentally devoid of authenticity. The claim that real, organic human-generated content is in rapid decline, replaced by AI-generated material designed to appear human, highlights concerns about the loss of genuine engagement online. While there is no empirical evidence to fully support these claims, the rise of AI-generated content in various online spaces provides a compelling backdrop for these theories. This essay explores the key claims of the Dead Internet Theory, examining how the internet has transformed, the implications of AI content generation, and the broader consequences for online culture and communication.

The Rise of AI-Generated Content and Bots

One of the central assertions of the Dead Internet Theory is that the internet's organic, human-driven content is quickly being replaced by AI-generated material. AI technologies have advanced rapidly over the past decade, with systems like OpenAI's GPT-3 and DALL·E, Google's BERT, and various other neural networks capable of creating text, images, and even videos that closely resemble those produced by humans. These AI tools are being used to produce vast amounts of content across social media platforms, news websites, forums, and even customer service chatbots, all designed to simulate human interaction and engagement.

For example, social media platforms are rife with AI-generated posts, comments, and messages. Bots, powered by AI algorithms, can produce convincing tweets, Facebook posts, and Instagram captions, engaging with real users and giving the illusion of organic interaction. This creates a scenario where the lines between real, human-generated content and AI-created content are becoming increasingly blurred. These bots can be used to amplify specific viewpoints, spread misinformation, or manipulate online conversations, leading to a virtual environment that feels more controlled and less genuine. Bots can flood comment sections with repetitive or scripted responses, thus overwhelming authentic interactions and reducing the overall quality of discourse.

This surge in AI-driven content is evident in the rise of "clickbait" articles, which are often written by AI to maximize engagement with the least amount of effort. These articles are crafted based on keyword optimization and algorithms designed to grab attention, rather than meaningful, well-researched writing. News outlets, particularly in the realm of business and sports, have adopted AI to generate articles on predictable topics such as earnings reports or game results. While these articles might be factually accurate, they often lack the depth, insight, or creativity that comes from human writers. Moreover, these kinds of AI-generated articles are often repetitive and rely heavily on trends and data, making them feel formulaic and impersonal.

The Decline of Human-Centered Engagement

According to the Dead Internet Theory, the prevalence of AI-generated content signals the death of real, human-centered engagement online. Social media and online forums, once vibrant spaces for individuals to connect, share ideas, and discuss topics of interest, are increasingly populated by AI-generated content that lacks the genuine, personal touch of human interaction.

Take, for example, the shift in online communities. In the early days of the internet, platforms like Reddit, forums, and early social media websites were hubs of genuine, human-driven conversations. People shared personal experiences, debated issues, and formed connections based on mutual interests. Today, however, many online spaces are overrun by bots that contribute to conversations, create fake posts, or amplify specific viewpoints. These bots are designed to mimic human conversation and appear as though they are genuine participants, but they are ultimately programmed to advance specific agendas or generate engagement for commercial purposes. As a result, the internet can feel less like a space for authentic interaction and more like a platform for automated communication.

Another key concern highlighted by proponents of the Dead Internet Theory is the increasing commercial influence over online content. As companies and advertisers deploy AI tools to control what users see, the content online becomes more tailored to profit motives rather than personal expression or genuine conversation. Personalized ads, promoted posts, and algorithmic feeds on platforms like Facebook and Instagram ensure that users are exposed to a constant stream of content that is engineered for engagement rather than authenticity. The human voice, once the driving force of internet content, now competes with sophisticated algorithms designed to maximize clicks and attention.

Furthermore, the rise of AI-generated content impacts the quality of the content itself. Unlike human creators, who bring personal experiences, emotions, and insights into their work, AI-generated content is created based on patterns, data, and algorithms. It often lacks the unique perspectives, creativity, and individuality that come with human input. While AI can generate grammatically correct sentences and convincing articles, it cannot replicate the complexity of human thought, emotion, or cultural context. The result is content that, while polished, feels hollow and generic.

The Implications of a Dead Internet: Misinformation and Control

The proliferation of AI-generated content does not merely affect the authenticity of online interactions; it also has significant implications for misinformation, political manipulation, and the overall quality of discourse. In the past, the internet was a space where a diversity of voices could emerge, and organic content from humans could create opportunities for learning, sharing, and innovation. However, as AI-generated material increasingly dominates online spaces, the authenticity of the content is compromised, making it more difficult for users to discern between truth and falsehood.

One of the most concerning aspects of this shift is the rise of AI-driven misinformation. Since bots and AI tools can generate content at an unprecedented scale, they can be used to flood the internet with misleading or false information, sometimes with malicious intent. For instance, AI-generated fake news articles, social media posts, and videos can spread false narratives, manipulate public opinion, or undermine trust in credible news sources. In some cases, deepfakes — AI-generated videos that can convincingly alter a person's speech or appearance — can be used to deceive audiences and influence elections or public opinion.

Moreover, as AI becomes better at mimicking human behavior, it also poses a risk of manipulation. Algorithms that are designed to increase user engagement can exploit human cognitive biases, encouraging users to engage with content that confirms their pre-existing beliefs, rather than challenging them or presenting diverse perspectives. This can exacerbate polarization, as users are more likely to be exposed to content that aligns with their views and less likely to encounter content that challenges their thinking. As AI-generated content fills the internet, it could lead to a narrowing of perspectives, creating echo chambers where misinformation thrives.

Counterarguments: AI as a Tool, Not a Replacement

While the Dead Internet Theory paints a grim picture of the internet's future, it is important to acknowledge that AI-generated content is not inherently harmful or an automatic replacement for human creativity. In fact, AI has the potential to enhance human engagement online by enabling faster content creation, automating repetitive tasks, and assisting with content curation. For instance, AI-generated articles on routine topics like stock market reports or sports scores can free up human journalists to focus on more in-depth investigative reporting. Additionally, AI chatbots are commonly used in customer service to provide quick, efficient responses, improving the overall user experience.

Furthermore, AI-generated content can be an aid to creators, not a replacement. Writers, artists, and musicians are already using AI tools to enhance their work, sparking new forms of collaboration between humans and machines. AI's role, then, should be viewed not as a threat to organic content but as an opportunity to expand the ways in which humans interact with and create digital material.

A Balanced Future for the Internet

The Dead Internet Theory's claim that real human-generated organic content is in rapid decline due to the rise of AI-generated material raises important questions about the future of online engagement. While AI-generated content undoubtedly has a growing presence in various forms of media, it is important to recognize the potential for collaboration between human creators and AI tools. The key to maintaining authenticity in the digital age lies in ensuring that AI is used ethically and responsibly, with safeguards in place to prevent the manipulation of online discourse and the spread of misinformation.

As AI continues to evolve, it is essential that society strikes a balance between leveraging its capabilities and preserving the human touch that has made the internet such a dynamic and engaging space. By doing so, we can ensure that the internet remains a platform for authentic communication, creativity, and diverse perspectives, rather than becoming a digital landscape dominated by bots and automated content.

EVIDENCE FOR THE DEAD INTERNET THEORY: BOT ACTIVITY ON SOCIAL MEDIA PLATFORMS

The Dead Internet Theory posits that the internet, once a thriving space for genuine human interaction, is now increasingly dominated by artificial intelligence (AI) and bot-driven content, leading to a decline in authentic, organic human-generated engagement. One of the key elements of this theory is the growing presence of bots on social media platforms like Twitter, Instagram, and Facebook, where automated accounts are used to generate fake content, manipulate discussions, and amplify specific agendas. This essay explores the evidence supporting the Dead Internet Theory, specifically focusing on bot activity on social media platforms, backed by statistics and studies that highlight the increasing prevalence of fake accounts and the implications for online discourse.

The Rise of Bot Activity on Social Media

Bots are automated programs that mimic human behavior on social media platforms, performing tasks such as posting content, liking posts, following accounts, and engaging in conversations. While bots have legitimate uses, such as automating customer service or content curation, their increasing use in social media manipulation, misinformation campaigns, and the amplification of certain viewpoints is a growing concern.

The scale of bot activity on social media is staggering. According to a study by the Massachusetts Institute of Technology (MIT), around 15% of Twitter accounts are believed to be bots. In 2021, Twitter itself reported that approximately

5% of its daily active users were automated accounts, a number that has likely grown in the years since. The total number of fake accounts on Twitter is estimated to be in the tens of millions. These bots are used for various purposes, from spreading political misinformation to promoting products and services. In fact, bots were found to be responsible for as much as 50% of the posts related to political topics during major elections, particularly in the United States.

On Instagram, bots are similarly prevalent. A 2020 report by the cybersecurity firm "HypeAuditor" found that approximately 30% of Instagram accounts with over 1,000 followers are either fake or inactive. These fake accounts are used to artificially inflate follower counts, engage in targeted advertising campaigns, and manipulate the perception of social media influence. Many companies have even begun to hire influencers with large but fake followings, further blurring the lines between genuine human engagement and bot-driven content.

The Purpose and Impact of Bots on Social Media

Bots on social media are employed for various purposes, some of which are benign, such as automating mundane tasks, while others are more insidious. One of the most concerning uses of bots is the manipulation of public opinion through the dissemination of fake news and misinformation. Bots can rapidly spread false or misleading information by generating large volumes of tweets or posts that appear to come from real users, making the content seem more credible and widespread than it truly is.

During the 2016 U.S. presidential election, for example, it was revealed that Russian-backed bots were used to influence political discussions on Twitter, Facebook, and Instagram. A report from the Senate Intelligence Committee found that over 80,000 posts from Russian bots were shared on Facebook alone, reaching millions of users and influencing political opinions during the election period. Bots on Twitter were used to amplify divisive political messages, spreading disinformation and creating artificial polarization. Studies showed that fake news spread by bots was 70% more likely to be shared than true news, raising concerns about the role of automated accounts in shaping public discourse.

Bots also contribute to the proliferation of echo chambers, where users are exposed to content that reinforces their existing beliefs rather than challenging them. Algorithms on social media platforms prioritize content that generates engagement, which often leads to the amplification of extreme viewpoints, whether political, social, or cultural. By artificially inflating the reach of specific content, bots can further isolate individuals within ideological bubbles, making it harder for them to encounter diverse perspectives. This, in turn, diminishes the authenticity of online conversations and the diversity of opinions that were once more readily accessible in the early days of the internet.

Evidence from Studies and Statistics

Numerous studies have documented the growing presence of bots on social media platforms, providing concrete evidence for the Dead Internet Theory's claims regarding the decline of human-generated content. A 2019 study by the Oxford Internet Institute revealed that political bots were increasingly used during elections across the world, particularly in countries like the U.S., the U.K., and Brazil. The study found that automated accounts generated a significant portion of the conversation surrounding election-related hashtags, often spreading false information or amplifying partisan viewpoints. In Brazil's 2018 presidential election, for instance, bots were responsible for 30% of the posts related to political candidates, influencing the public conversation in ways that distorted the electoral process.

On Twitter, the scale of bot activity has led to concerns about the credibility of online interactions. A 2018 report by the cybersecurity company "F5 Networks" found that nearly 30% of the interactions on Twitter related to political topics were generated by bots. These bots are not only used to manipulate public opinion but also to boost the popularity of specific topics, trends, or hashtags. This activity makes it more difficult for real users to discern what content is genuinely popular or widely discussed, as bots often skew trends to appear more influential than they are.

Further evidence of the bot-driven manipulation of social media can be found in the 2020 study by the cybersecurity firm "ZeroFOX," which found that 16% of all Twitter accounts involved in discussing the COVID-19 pandemic were bots. These accounts were used to spread misleading information about the virus, vaccines, and public health guidelines. The bots were able to spread false narratives at a speed and scale that would have been impossible for human users alone, significantly contributing to the infodemic surrounding the pandemic.

Consequences for Social Media and Public Discourse

The increasing number of bots on social media has profound implications for the way we interact online. As more fake accounts and automated content flood these platforms, the authenticity of online interactions is undermined. Users are often exposed to content that is artificially amplified, making it more difficult to discern real human opinions from content generated by algorithms or automated bots. This leads to a decline in the quality of discourse, as individuals may be influenced by content that is engineered to appear genuine but is, in reality, manufactured.

Furthermore, the manipulation of online content by bots and automated systems also raises concerns about privacy, security, and misinformation. Bots can be used to gather personal data from social media platforms, spreading malicious links or phishing scams. As social media platforms become increasingly monetized, the rise of fake accounts also undermines the authenticity of social media marketing, as brands may unknowingly pay for influencer promotions based on inflated follower counts or fake engagement.

Considerations

The growing presence of bots on social media platforms like Twitter and Instagram provides significant evidence for the Dead Internet Theory's claim that real human-generated content is in rapid decline. The increasing manipulation of online conversations by bots, coupled with studies showing the rising number of fake accounts, paints a concerning picture of the digital landscape. As bots flood social media with automated content, the authenticity of online interactions is compromised, and users are exposed to distorted narratives and manipulated discussions. While bots can serve legitimate purposes in automating tasks, their increasing influence on social media raises critical questions about the future of online engagement and the role of artificial intelligence in shaping our digital reality. Addressing these concerns will require concerted efforts from policymakers, tech companies, and users to ensure that the internet remains a space for authentic, human-driven content and meaningful interaction.

EVIDENCE FOR THE DEAD INTERNET THEORY: THE RISE OF AI-GENERATED CONTENT

The Dead Internet Theory suggests that the internet, once a vibrant space for human interaction and authentic content, is increasingly dominated by artificial intelligence (AI)-generated material. This content, though designed to mimic human writing and behavior, is ultimately devoid of the personal touch, creativity, and depth that come from genuine human expression. The theory claims that AI-driven content has overtaken organic human-generated material, filling the internet with articles, blog posts, and social media posts that appear human but lack authenticity. This essay will explore the growing prevalence of AI-generated content, highlighting examples from news articles, blogs, and social media, and examining the impact of this shift on the quality of online discourse and information.

AI-Generated News Articles and Content

One of the most prominent areas where AI-generated content has taken hold is in the field of news reporting. With the rise of machine learning models like OpenAI's GPT-3 and similar AI technologies, media outlets have begun to utilize automated systems to generate news articles at scale. AI is particularly effective in generating routine, data-driven stories such as weather reports, sports summaries, financial news, and even some political coverage. These AI systems can quickly analyze vast amounts of data, identify key trends, and produce articles in a fraction of the time it would take a human journalist.

For example, in 2018, the Associated Press (AP) began using an AI program to generate thousands of quarterly earnings reports. The program, called Wordsmith, generates data-heavy articles by parsing financial data and then automatically constructing coherent narratives around it. These articles are published without human oversight and have the appearance of traditional journalism. However, despite their technical accuracy, these AI-generated articles often lack the nuance, critical analysis, or investigative depth that a human journalist would bring to the story. While they provide essential information, they do little to engage readers on a deeper level, missing the human touch that can make news reporting compelling.

AI's role in the production of news articles has raised concerns about the quality of information being disseminated. Critics argue that while AI can efficiently produce large volumes of content, it struggles to contextualize complex issues, interpret subtle nuances, and add human insight. In a world where the volume of content is prioritized over its quality, the proliferation of AI-generated news risks diluting the richness of journalism, leading to a more superficial and formulaic approach to information sharing.

AI-Generated Blog Posts and Web Content

AI-generated content is also becoming prevalent in the realm of blogs, websites, and SEO (Search Engine Optimization) content. Websites designed to attract traffic often use AI to generate blog posts optimized for search engines, ensuring that they rank highly on Google and other search platforms. These posts, often composed of generic, keyword-optimized content, mimic human writing by adhering to common writing patterns but lack originality and personal voice.

Tools like Jasper (formerly Jarvis) and Copy.ai have become popular among content marketers and bloggers. These AI writing assistants use machine learning algorithms to create blog posts, product descriptions, and advertisements based on minimal input from users. The AI generates content that follows the input guidelines, such as writing a blog post about "the benefits of sustainable living," but often the resulting text is generic and repetitive. While the writing may pass as human-like at first glance, it lacks the distinctive voice and perspective that comes from personal experience or expertise. It may provide useful information, but it lacks the depth, unique insights, or personal anecdotes that make content truly resonate with readers.

Furthermore, AI-generated content is often structured to prioritize keywords and SEO best practices rather than genuine human engagement. The primary goal of such content is to rank high in search results, rather than to offer deep, meaningful engagement with a topic. As a result, readers may encounter a vast amount of content that appears to be informative or valuable but, in reality, is little more than a repackaged version of surface-level information that is designed for algorithmic success. The proliferation of such content raises questions about the authenticity and purpose of much of what is published on the internet today.

AI-Generated Social Media Content

Social media platforms are another space where AI-generated content has become increasingly common. AI bots are being deployed to generate posts, comments, and even entire social media profiles that mimic human behavior. These bots can automatically post content at specific times, like and share posts, and interact with users to increase engagement on a platform. While some of these bots are created for benign purposes, such as marketing and customer service, others are used to manipulate conversations, promote false narratives, and create the illusion of popular support for certain ideas or brands.

AI-generated social media content is often designed to mimic human interaction in ways that are difficult for users to distinguish from real posts. For example, AI bots can generate comments on Instagram posts or Twitter threads that appear to be genuine user engagement. These comments may include likes, shares, or replies that amplify the visibility of particular posts, thus influencing which content gains traction. While these bots can create the illusion of a lively and diverse conversation, the reality is that much of what is shared and discussed on social media is not created by real humans but by automated systems designed to mimic human behavior.

The impact of AI-generated social media content is particularly concerning when it comes to the spread of misinformation and the creation of fake influence. During political elections, for example, AI bots have been used to simulate public opinion, making certain political figures or ideas seem more popular than they truly are. By generating thousands of fake posts and comments, these bots can create a false sense of consensus, manipulating users into thinking that a particular viewpoint is widely supported. This phenomenon has raised alarm over the authenticity of online discussions and the potential for AI to be used to sway public opinion in undemocratic ways.

The Lack of Authenticity in AI-Generated Content

While AI-generated content can be remarkably convincing on the surface, it often lacks the depth, nuance, and personal experience that characterize authentic human expression. Human writers draw from their own experiences, emotions, and insights, creating content that resonates with readers on a deeper level. In contrast, AI-generated content is based on patterns and algorithms, rather than lived experience. As a result, AI-generated material tends to be formulaic, shallow, and lacking in personal connection.

For example, an AI-generated blog post about mental health may contain accurate information about symptoms and treatment options, but it may lack the empathy or personal understanding that a human writer can bring to the topic. A human writer might share a personal story, offer advice based on their own experiences, or convey a sense of understanding that helps readers feel seen and heard. AI-generated content, on the other hand, is often clinical and impersonal, offering information without the emotional depth that makes human communication meaningful.

Similarly, AI-generated news articles or social media posts may present facts in a clear and concise manner, but they often fail to capture the complexity of human emotions, social dynamics, or cultural context. AI lacks the ability to understand subtle shifts in tone or the emotional weight of certain topics. As a result, AI-generated content may come across as sterile or detached, offering information without the rich human perspective that makes content truly engaging.

The Diminishing Human Element in Online Content

The Dead Internet Theory posits that the internet is increasingly dominated by AI-generated content, replacing organic human-driven material and leading to a decline in the authenticity and depth of online interactions. While AI has proven to be an effective tool for generating large volumes of content across various platforms, including news articles, blog posts, and social media interactions, this content often lacks the personal experience, creativity, and emotional depth that characterize authentic human expression. As AI-driven content continues to fill the digital landscape, the authenticity of online communication is at risk, raising concerns about the future of online discourse. While AI-generated content can serve useful functions, such as automating routine tasks or generating data-driven reports, its growing dominance highlights the need for greater emphasis on preserving genuine human engagement in the digital world.

EVIDENCE FOR THE DEAD INTERNET THEORY: SEARCH ENGINES AND ALGORITHMIC MANIPULATION

The Dead Internet Theory proposes that the internet, once a vibrant space for authentic human interaction and user-generated content, is now increasingly dominated by automated systems, bots, and AI-generated material. As part of this shift, algorithms controlling search engines, social media platforms, and content recommendation systems are playing a crucial role in shaping what users see and interact with online. These algorithms increasingly prioritize content generated by AI, paid entities, or commercial interests over organic human voices. This essay explores the evidence for the Dead Internet Theory regarding the growing influence of search engine algorithms, social media algorithms, and recommendation systems, focusing on how these systems push AI-generated content and corporate-driven narratives while sidelining authentic, human-driven content.

The Growing Influence of Search Engine Algorithms

Search engines, such as Google, have long been the gateway through which users access information online. However, over the past decade, search engine algorithms have undergone significant changes that have shifted the nature of online content. Instead of offering users a broad range of diverse and organic sources, search engine algorithms now prioritize content from paid entities, large corporations, and AI-generated sources.

Google's algorithm, for example, is designed to provide users with the most relevant and authoritative information. However, the definition of "relevant" has evolved to favor commercial and SEO-optimized content. SEO (Search Engine Optimization) has become a multi-billion-dollar industry that aims to manipulate search engine algorithms to ensure that content from specific sources ranks higher than others. While this often results in high-quality, well-researched content being promoted, it also creates an environment where corporate websites, paid content, and AI-generated articles have a better chance of appearing at the top of search results, even when the information is not the most relevant or accurate.

A 2020 study by the Columbia Journalism Review found that more than 40% of the top results for popular searches on Google were sponsored or paid content. Additionally, content marketing companies and AI-driven tools are now able to generate articles optimized for search engines, filling web pages with AI-written blog posts designed to rank highly on Google. These pieces may appear on search results, but they often lack depth, nuance, or a genuine personal voice. Instead, they are carefully crafted to meet the algorithm's criteria, such as keyword usage, user engagement, and SEO best practices.

In the context of the Dead Internet Theory, this trend highlights the diminishing role of organic human voices in search engine results. As search engines become more focused on ranking paid or SEO-optimized content, the diverse range of human-generated content that once characterized the internet becomes increasingly invisible. This shift prioritizes commercial and AI-driven voices, gradually sidelining authentic, independent creators and reducing the authenticity of online information.

Social Media Algorithms and Their Role in Content Amplification

Social media platforms like Facebook, Instagram, Twitter, and YouTube are also governed by sophisticated algorithms that determine what content users see in their feeds. These algorithms are designed to prioritize content that generates high levels of engagement, such as likes, shares, comments, and views. In doing so, they increasingly amplify content that is tailored to fit specific user interests, commercial objectives, or AI-generated trends, while sidelining content that might reflect a more diverse range of human experiences or opinions.

One significant concern is the role of paid content and influencer marketing in social media algorithms. Companies and individuals can pay for boosted posts or advertisements that receive priority placement in users' feeds. This has led to a situation where social media users are often exposed to content from corporations, commercial entities, and influencers, rather than organic posts created by individuals. A report by the marketing platform Hootsuite found that 72% of all social media ad spending in 2020 was directed toward Facebook and Instagram, platforms that use algorithmic systems to target users with highly personalized ads. As a result, much of the content users interact with is either sponsored or driven by AI-based targeting mechanisms designed to maximize engagement and profit.

The increasing automation of content creation and curation also plays a significant role in shaping what appears on social media. AI-powered tools can now generate captions, hashtags, and even full posts that mimic human voices but are, in reality, engineered to align with specific commercial interests or algorithmic preferences. These AI-generated posts often lack the authenticity of organic human content, as they are not driven by personal experience, genuine interest, or creativity but by the goal of achieving algorithmic success.

Moreover, algorithms on platforms like YouTube often prioritize videos that garner high view counts or engagement, which often results in the amplification of sensational or viral content. This trend has led to the rise of clickbait, misinformation, and polarizing narratives. A 2021 study by the Pew Research Center found that 62% of U.S. adults believe social media platforms do more to divide than to unify society, partly due to the algorithmic amplification of extreme or divisive content. This further underscores how the power of algorithms and AI-driven curation can create echo chambers, where users are exposed to a narrow range of ideas and perspectives while missing out on more diverse and authentic voices.

Content Recommendation Systems and Their Influence on the Digital Landscape

Content recommendation systems, which are used by platforms like YouTube, Netflix, Spotify, and TikTok, also play a significant role in shaping the internet as we know it today. These systems use sophisticated AI algorithms to suggest videos, songs, articles, and other content based on a user's past behavior, preferences, and interactions. While these systems are designed to enhance user experience by offering personalized content, they have also contributed to the dominance of AI-generated material and the prioritization of commercial or algorithmically optimized content over human voices.

One major impact of recommendation systems is the algorithmic reinforcement of commercial and corporate-driven content. For instance, YouTube's recommendation system tends to promote videos from channels that generate high levels of engagement or are optimized for viral success, rather than videos from independent creators or those with a more niche, non-commercial focus. This leads to a situation where algorithmic preferences often dictate what content becomes visible, rather than the quality or authenticity of the content itself. In the context of the Dead Internet Theory, this dynamic reflects how platforms prioritize material generated by paid entities or AI systems over content from genuine, organic human creators.

Additionally, recommendation systems can sometimes propagate misinformation or conspiracy theories. For example, in the aftermath of the 2020 U.S. presidential election, research showed that YouTube's recommendation algorithm was frequently suggesting videos related to election fraud and misinformation, often from politically biased or unreliable sources. While these videos were not directly AI-generated, the algorithmic amplification of content based on user behavior helped spread misleading narratives, further diminishing the quality of online discourse and public trust in the digital landscape.

TikTok, another platform that relies heavily on its recommendation algorithm, has been criticized for promoting viral trends, including AI-generated videos, over content that might offer more authentic or original expressions. These trends often mimic human behavior but are driven by AI-powered algorithms designed to optimize user engagement. The result is an online environment where users are more likely to engage with content that has been curated to maximize views or interactions rather than material that is genuinely meaningful, diverse, or human-centered.

The Growing Role of Algorithms in the Decline of Organic Content

The rise of search engine algorithms, social media algorithms, and content recommendation systems has contributed significantly to the decline of organic, human-generated content, providing ample evidence for the Dead Internet Theory. These algorithms prioritize content that is SEO-optimized, paid for, or generated by AI, often at the expense of more diverse, authentic, and human-driven voices. As commercial interests and automated systems continue to dominate the digital landscape, the ability of users to encounter genuine, meaningful content becomes increasingly diminished. The growing influence of algorithmic manipulation underscores the need for a more transparent and ethical approach to content curation on the internet, one that values authentic human engagement over commercial interests and AI-driven automation. The future of the internet may depend on efforts to reclaim space for genuine human voices amidst the growing dominance of algorithmically curated and AI-generated material.

THE ROLE OF BIG TECH COMPANIES IN THE MONOPOLIZATION OF THE INTERNET: THE IMPACT OF GOOGLE, META, AND AMAZON ON DIGITAL INFRASTRUCTURE AND HUMAN AGENCY

The internet, once a decentralized space that allowed for diverse voices, creativity, and innovation, has gradually become dominated by a few large corporations—primarily Google, Meta (formerly Facebook), and Amazon. These tech giants control much of the digital infrastructure that powers online interactions, from search engines and social media to e-commerce and cloud computing services. As these companies expand their influence, concerns about the monopolization of the internet and its impact on human agency and independent voices grow. This essay explores the role of big tech companies in monopolizing the internet and examines the consequences of their dominance on free expression, access to information, and the ability for independent creators to thrive.

Google's Dominance in Search and Digital Advertising

Google is arguably the most dominant player in the digital world, with its search engine processing over 90% of global search queries as of 2023. The company has effectively monopolized the way we access information online, shaping the flow of knowledge and news. Google's dominance in search engines directly influences what people know, what they see, and what they engage with, giving it unprecedented control over public discourse and the dissemination of information.

Beyond search, Google also controls a significant portion of digital advertising. Through its advertising platform, Google Ads, the company holds a substantial share of the global online advertising market. This influence extends across other platforms, including YouTube, which Google owns, and other websites that rely on Google's ad network for revenue. The search and advertising systems are deeply interconnected, and Google's algorithms prioritize content based on commercial interests, often pushing paid content and promoting corporate-sponsored narratives over organic voices. This is a key aspect of the monopolization of the internet: Google's algorithms dictate which content rises to the top of search results, effectively narrowing the scope of information that users encounter.

This concentration of power undermines the diversity of voices online, as smaller or independent creators often find it difficult to gain visibility. The pursuit of SEO optimization becomes essential for anyone seeking to be noticed on Google, pushing content creators to conform to algorithmic rules that favor commercial and paid interests. This has led to a homogeneity of content online, where corporate-controlled narratives are more likely to dominate and independent voices struggle to break through.

Meta's Control of Social Media and User Data

Meta, which owns Facebook, Instagram, and WhatsApp, controls a significant portion of global social media interaction, with billions of active users across its platforms. As a result, Meta has immense power over how information is shared, discussed, and consumed in the digital space. With algorithms determining what users see in their feeds, Meta's platforms prioritize content that generates engagement—such as likes, shares, and comments—often amplifying sensational or divisive content. This not only limits the diversity of content but also shapes the way users perceive reality.

Meta's control over social media is compounded by its extensive data collection practices. The company collects vast amounts of personal data from its users, which it uses to refine its algorithms, target advertisements, and influence what content appears in users' feeds. This practice has led to increasing concerns about privacy, with critics arguing that Meta's business model relies on exploiting personal data for profit. The extensive surveillance of user behavior creates a feedback loop where users are bombarded with tailored content that reinforces existing biases and reduces exposure to diverse perspectives.

The monopolistic nature of Meta's social media empire poses a significant threat to independent voices. Smaller platforms or alternative social media networks struggle to compete with Meta's reach, and users are often reluctant to migrate to new platforms that lack the same level of social integration and content-sharing capabilities. The result is a digital ecosystem dominated by a few large companies that control both the flow of information and the ways in which users interact with it. Independent creators, activists, and organizations often find themselves sidelined, as their content is less likely to be promoted by Meta's algorithms or to generate the engagement necessary for visibility.

Furthermore, Meta's content moderation policies— often opaque and subject to criticism—have raised concerns about censorship and bias. By determining what is allowed and what is not on its platforms, Meta wields significant power over the speech of billions of people worldwide. This centralized control limits the free exchange of ideas, especially for those whose voices do not align with the mainstream or corporate narratives promoted by the platform.

Amazon's Control of E-Commerce and Cloud Infrastructure

Amazon, another major player in the monopolization of the internet, has reshaped the digital economy by controlling a significant portion of global e-commerce and cloud computing infrastructure. With Amazon Web Services (AWS), the company powers much of the cloud infrastructure that supports the internet, from hosting websites and applications to providing storage and computing power for businesses. AWS has become the backbone for countless companies, including other tech giants like Netflix and Facebook. This gives Amazon unparalleled influence over the functioning of the internet itself, as any disruption in AWS can have far-reaching effects on global online services.

In addition to its control over cloud infrastructure, Amazon has also cornered the online retail market. As of 2023, Amazon accounts for nearly half of all online sales in the United States. The company's dominance in e-commerce has stifled competition, particularly for smaller, independent retailers who cannot compete with Amazon's vast selection, competitive pricing, and logistics infrastructure. Many small businesses are forced to rely on Amazon's platform to reach consumers, which often means sacrificing control over their branding, customer relationships, and profit margins.

Furthermore, Amazon's influence extends beyond e-commerce and cloud computing to its growing role in digital content. The company owns and operates platforms like Amazon Prime Video, Audible, and Kindle, consolidating its power over the distribution of digital media. Amazon's ability to control the availability and pricing of digital products, from books to movies, further exemplifies its monopolistic power and its impact on creators and consumers alike. For independent creators, especially those in the book publishing industry, Amazon's dominance can make or break a career. Authors are often forced to sell through Amazon's platform, giving the company significant control over their revenue and visibility.

The rise of Amazon and its monopolistic practices is an example of how centralized control of digital infrastructure limits human agency. As businesses, content creators, and consumers become increasingly dependent on Amazon's services, they lose the freedom to operate outside of Amazon's reach. This concentration of power restricts the diversity of voices and entrepreneurial opportunities available on the internet.

The Consequences of Internet Monopolization on Human Agency

The monopolization of the internet by a few large corporations like Google, Meta, and Amazon has profound implications for human agency and the diversity of voices online. First and foremost, these companies' control over digital infrastructure limits access to information. Algorithms designed to prioritize certain content—whether through search engines, social media feeds, or e-commerce platforms—reduce the visibility of independent creators, alternative perspectives, and niche topics. This leads to a more homogenous online environment, where corporate interests, paid content, and algorithmically optimized material dominate.

Moreover, the centralization of power in a few large companies reduces the ability of individuals to shape their digital experiences. Users are increasingly reliant on algorithms that determine what they see, read, and purchase. In the context of social media, for example, users no longer have full control over their feeds; instead, they are presented with content that fits predefined patterns of engagement and profit. This diminishes the agency of individuals, limiting their capacity to discover diverse viewpoints, engage with independent content creators, or even challenge mainstream narratives.

The monopolization of the internet also leads to the erosion of privacy and data security. With companies like Meta and Google collecting vast amounts of personal data, individuals have little control over how their information is used, shared, or sold. This raises concerns about surveillance and the exploitation of personal data for profit.

Considerations

The monopolization of the internet by big tech companies such as Google, Meta, and Amazon has significant consequences for human agency and the diversity of voices online. By controlling critical digital infrastructure, these companies shape the flow of information, limit access to independent content, and prioritize commercial interests over organic human engagement. As these tech giants continue to expand their influence, it is crucial to address the monopolistic practices that undermine the open, decentralized nature of the internet and to advocate for policies that promote diversity, competition, and individual freedom in the digital space. Only by addressing these issues can the internet once again become a platform that truly empowers human voices and creativity.

THE ROLE OF BIG TECH COMPANIES IN CENSORSHIP AND CONTENT CONTROL: HOW TECH GIANTS MANIPULATE WHAT USERS SEE AND ENGAGE WITH

The internet has evolved into a vital space for information sharing, communication, entertainment, and activism. However, as the digital landscape has grown, so too has the influence of big tech companies—particularly Google, Meta (formerly Facebook), Amazon, and Twitter. These companies have consolidated control over vast portions of the online experience, shaping how users access content and engage with one another. With this power, these tech giants not only curate the flow of information but also exert significant influence over what content is visible, what is suppressed, and who has the opportunity to participate in the digital discourse. This control over information, often framed as censorship, has raised concerns about the erosion of free speech, the manipulation of public opinion, and the creation of a curated version of the internet that serves the interests of these corporations.

The Power of Algorithms and Content Moderation

At the heart of big tech companies' content control lies the use of algorithms and content moderation policies. These companies employ algorithms designed to determine which content is most likely to engage users and keep them on their platforms. For example, social media platforms like Facebook and Instagram use algorithms that prioritize content that generates high levels of engagement, such as likes, shares, comments, and click-through rates. Similarly, YouTube's recommendation algorithm suggests videos based on user behavior, preferences, and engagement patterns. While these algorithms aim to enhance user experience, they also have the unintended effect of amplifying certain types of content—often sensational, controversial, or divisive—while minimizing others.

In addition to algorithmic manipulation, big tech companies also exercise control over content through direct moderation. Content moderation typically involves removing posts or accounts that violate platform guidelines, such as content deemed harmful, misleading, or offensive. However, the implementation of these guidelines is often controversial, with critics arguing that content moderation practices have been inconsistent, biased, or overly restrictive. For instance, platforms like Facebook and Twitter have been accused of suppressing certain political views or dissenting opinions, while allowing harmful or misleading content to thrive.

This dual mechanism of algorithmic curation and content moderation creates a curated version of the internet— one that prioritizes content that aligns with the platform's goals, whether those are maximizing engagement, promoting advertisers, or adhering to political or social agendas. In doing so, tech companies not only shape the information users see but also dictate the boundaries of acceptable discourse.

Censorship Through Algorithmic Prioritization and De-prioritization

One of the most subtle yet powerful ways that big tech companies engage in censorship is through algorithmic prioritization and de-prioritization. Algorithms on platforms like Google and Facebook determine which content rises to the top of search results or appears first in users' feeds. This process inherently involves a form of gatekeeping, as only content that fits the algorithmic criteria—such as high engagement rates or alignment with advertiser interests—gets visibility.

In the case of Google, the company controls the search engine results that billions of users rely on to access information. The algorithms that dictate which websites appear at the top of the search results are designed to favor content that has been SEO-optimized, commercialized, or sponsored. While this results in more accurate, user-friendly searches in many cases, it also means that organic, independent, or non-commercial content often gets buried. Furthermore, paid content—whether through search ads or sponsored articles—often appears at the top of results, meaning that users are more likely to encounter corporate, commercial, or AI-generated content rather than diverse perspectives or independent voices.

Social media platforms also engage in algorithmic censorship by promoting content that triggers emotional responses or generates engagement. For instance, Facebook's algorithm tends to prioritize emotionally charged content, including polarizing posts and sensational headlines. While this maximizes user interaction, it also contributes to the spread of misinformation, propaganda, and biased narratives. At the same time, the algorithm pushes down content that may be nuanced, thoughtful, or critical of mainstream narratives, as these types of posts often do not generate the same level of engagement.

This system of algorithmic manipulation has serious implications for the way users engage with content. It leads to a situation where what is seen online is increasingly shaped by corporate and commercial interests rather than being a true reflection of the full spectrum of opinions and information available. For instance, social media platforms have been accused of favoring content that aligns with particular political ideologies or corporate agendas, leading to an online ecosystem where certain viewpoints are systematically suppressed or ignored.

The Politics of Content Moderation and Censorship

In addition to algorithmic control, big tech companies exercise direct influence over what content is allowed on their platforms through content moderation policies. These policies are designed to remove harmful or illegal content, such as hate speech, misinformation, or incitement to violence. While this is a necessary function to protect users and maintain a safe online environment, the line between legitimate content moderation and censorship can be blurred.

One of the most controversial aspects of content moderation is the perceived political bias inherent in the enforcement of platform guidelines. Social media platforms like Facebook and Twitter have faced criticism for selectively removing content that challenges mainstream political views or supports alternative political movements. For example, conservative users and right-wing figures have often accused platforms of disproportionately flagging or removing their content, alleging bias against their ideological views. Similarly, liberal or progressive voices have criticized platforms for allowing harmful misinformation or conspiracy theories to flourish without sufficient moderation, especially during high-stakes political events such as elections.

The power of these companies to censor content has become particularly evident during periods of political unrest or crises. During the 2020 U.S. presidential election, for example, Facebook and Twitter took unprecedented steps to curb the spread of misinformation by fact-checking and flagging posts related to voter fraud and election results. While these actions were taken with the goal of maintaining the integrity of the electoral process, they also sparked a heated debate about the role of tech companies in shaping public opinion and interfering with political discourse. In some cases, users argued that content moderation policies were not being applied consistently, leaving certain forms of misinformation unchecked or removing content that did not violate any clear guidelines.

This political dimension of content moderation raises questions about the role of tech giants as digital gatekeepers. With the vast amounts of data they collect on users, tech companies have the power to shape not only what users see but also how they think, feel, and vote. When this power is used to suppress certain political viewpoints or narratives, it can have a chilling effect on free speech and limit the diversity of ideas that are able to circulate online.

Corporate Interests and Commercial Censorship

While content moderation is often framed as a means of protecting users, it is also deeply intertwined with corporate interests. Big tech companies, as private entities, are driven by profit, and their business models are largely centered around maximizing user engagement and advertising revenue. This often leads to the prioritization of commercial content over organic, independent voices.

For example, YouTube's content moderation policies have been accused of demonetizing or de-prioritizing content that does not align with advertiser interests. Many content creators—especially those who create niche, controversial, or political content—have reported that their videos are demonetized or removed without clear explanation, limiting their ability to monetize their work. This kind of commercial censorship ensures that content creators are incentivized to conform to mainstream, advertiser-friendly narratives rather than pursuing independent or alternative ideas.

Moreover, the vast network of paid ads, sponsored content, and influencer marketing on platforms like Instagram and TikTok often blurs the line between organic and commercial content. These platforms' algorithms prioritize sponsored posts and branded content, which often appear seamlessly integrated into users' feeds, creating a curated digital experience that is heavily influenced by advertising dollars. This manipulation of content is designed to maximize profit at the expense of authentic, independent voices.

A Curated, Controlled, and Commercialized Internet

The role of big tech companies in censorship and content control is a key factor in the monopolization of the internet, which is now dominated by a few corporate giants. Through the use of algorithms, content moderation, and corporate-driven priorities, these companies control what users see, what they engage with, and how they interact with others online. This creates a curated version of the internet that often prioritizes sensational content, commercial interests, and politically favored narratives over authentic, diverse, and independent voices.

While there are legitimate concerns about the need for content moderation to protect users from harm, the increasing centralization of power in the hands of a few corporations has serious implications for free speech, the diversity of ideas, and the health of public discourse. As tech giants continue to refine their algorithms and enforce stricter content guidelines, it is crucial for regulators and users alike to consider the balance between protecting users from harmful content and safeguarding the free flow of ideas and information. The growing influence of big tech companies in shaping the digital landscape calls for a reevaluation of their role as gatekeepers and the potential consequences of their control over the information that defines our modern world.

THE ROLE OF BIG TECH COMPANIES IN DATA HARVESTING AND PRIVACY ISSUES: THE MANIPULATION OF USER BEHAVIOR AND THE EROSION OF THE FREE INTERNET

The internet has fundamentally transformed how individuals access information, communicate, and express themselves. However, with the rapid growth of digital platforms and the increasing consolidation of power in the hands of a few large tech companies, there has been a significant shift in how the internet operates. Today, many online spaces that were once designed for free expression and organic human interaction have been shaped by data harvesting and surveillance, leading to concerns about privacy, the manipulation of user behavior, and the loss of a free, open internet. Companies like Google, Meta (Facebook), Amazon, and others harvest vast amounts of personal data from their users, often without their full awareness or consent. This data is then used to curate content, manipulate user behavior, and target advertising, creating an ecosystem in which users are treated as products to be exploited. This essay explores the role of big tech companies in data harvesting, the associated privacy issues, and the growing concerns that the internet is no longer a free space for organic expression.

The Scale of Data Collection and Its Impact on Privacy

Big tech companies have built their business models around the collection of personal data. These companies have access to an unprecedented amount of information about users—ranging from personal details, browsing history, social media activity, location data, and even biometric data—thanks to their extensive networks of online platforms and services. Google, for example, collects data from its search engine,

YouTube, Gmail, Google Maps, and Android devices, while Facebook (Meta) collects data from its social media platforms, including Facebook, Instagram, WhatsApp, and Oculus. Amazon collects data from its e-commerce platform, Alexa, and AWS cloud services.

This data collection often occurs without users fully understanding the extent to which their information is being gathered or how it will be used. Although tech companies often present privacy policies and terms of service to inform users about data collection practices, these documents are often lengthy, complex, and difficult to understand. Many users simply click through them without reading or comprehending the details, leaving them unaware of the scale and scope of the data being harvested.

The result is a highly detailed digital profile of each user, built from their online activity, interactions, and preferences. This profile can include not only demographic information but also insights into an individual's interests, behaviors, and even their emotional state. In this sense, users have become products, with their data being monetized through targeted advertisements, content personalization, and other commercial ventures. However, this data collection raises significant privacy concerns. Despite the claims of companies to protect user privacy, data breaches, leaks, and the sale of personal data to third-party advertisers are frequent occurrences. This puts sensitive personal information at risk and underscores the limitations of trusting these companies with the vast amount of data they collect.

Manipulation of User Behavior through Data

The widespread collection of personal data is not simply for passive record-keeping; it is actively used to manipulate user behavior. Big tech companies have developed sophisticated algorithms that analyze user data and adjust the content, advertisements, and experiences they provide to maximize engagement, profit, and influence. These algorithms learn from users' past behaviors and use that information to predict what they are likely to click on, watch, or purchase next.

On social media platforms like Facebook and Instagram, the content users see in their feeds is influenced by engagement-based algorithms, which prioritize content that is likely to generate reactions such as likes, shares, or comments. By tailoring users' feeds to include content that they are most likely to engage with, these platforms create an environment where users are constantly exposed to content that reinforces their existing views and emotions. This process of content personalization can reinforce echo chambers, where users only encounter information and opinions that align with their own beliefs, further polarizing society and reducing exposure to diverse viewpoints.

In the context of advertising, big tech companies use data to create highly targeted ads that are personalized to each user. This level of targeting goes beyond demographic information to include psychographic data—insights into users' preferences, interests, and behaviors. For instance, an individual who frequently searches for fitness-related content may see advertisements for workout gear, supplements, or gym memberships, while someone who frequently engages with home improvement content may be targeted with ads for tools or furniture. While this type of advertising may seem convenient, it also raises questions about the extent to which users are being subtly influenced by personalized ads and the degree of control they have over their online experiences.

Moreover, the manipulation of user behavior extends beyond advertisements. Platforms like YouTube and TikTok use recommendation algorithms to suggest videos based on users' past interactions, creating a highly curated and personalized experience. However, this algorithmic personalization often promotes sensational or emotionally charged content to keep users engaged, which can lead to the proliferation of clickbait, misinformation, and polarized views. The result is a system where users are continuously guided toward content that is designed to capture their attention and reinforce particular behaviors, rather than offering a diverse and organic range of content.

The Loss of Organic Expression and the Commercialization of the Internet

The increasing reliance on data harvesting and algorithmic manipulation has led to a loss of organic expression on the internet. The internet was originally conceived as a free space for individuals to share ideas, create content, and engage with others. However, as big tech companies have gained control over the digital infrastructure, the internet has become more commercialized and less about authentic human interaction. In this new reality, the content users see is shaped not by personal choice or genuine interest, but by algorithms that prioritize engagement and profit.

For content creators, this shift has significant implications. The algorithms that govern platforms like Facebook, Instagram, and YouTube reward content that generates high levels of engagement, pushing creators to optimize their posts for visibility. This often means that creators must focus on producing content that is sensational, click-worthy, or aligned with mainstream trends, rather than content that is meaningful, thoughtful, or reflective of their authentic experiences. This commercialization of online platforms creates an environment where the most visible and successful creators are often those who can best cater to the whims of the algorithm, rather than those who produce original or thought-provoking work.

In addition, the pervasive collection of personal data has led to the rise of surveillance capitalism, where user behavior is constantly tracked and analyzed to maximize profit. This has created an online environment where users are not free to explore the internet on their own terms. Instead, their experiences are continually shaped by commercial interests and algorithmic biases, leading to a more homogenized, less authentic digital space. As platforms like Facebook and Instagram become increasingly designed to serve corporate interests, the space for independent voices to flourish has been significantly reduced.

Furthermore, as big tech companies accumulate more user data, they gain unprecedented power over individuals' digital lives. The manipulation of user behavior through targeted ads, curated content, and recommendations means that users are constantly being nudged toward particular products, ideas, or actions. This diminishes the autonomy of users, making them less free to engage with the internet on their own terms and more susceptible to the influence of corporate agendas.

The Erosion of Privacy and the Need for Regulation

The rise of data harvesting and manipulation of user behavior has contributed to a growing erosion of privacy on the internet. While some regulations, such as the European Union's General Data Protection Regulation (GDPR), have sought to address these issues by offering users more control over their data, the overall trend is one of increasing surveillance. Tech companies continue to collect vast amounts of data, often with little oversight, and use it to shape users' online experiences.

As the internet becomes less of a space for free expression and more of a commercialized platform controlled by a few large companies, the need for stronger regulation becomes more urgent. Privacy laws and regulations must be updated to reflect the realities of a digital world where personal data is constantly being collected, analyzed, and monetized. Additionally, there must be greater transparency around how data is used and how algorithms influence user behavior. Without these protections, the internet will continue to be a space where users' privacy is violated, and their behavior is manipulated by powerful tech companies.

Considerations

The role of big tech companies in data harvesting and the erosion of privacy has led to a fundamental shift in how the internet operates. What was once a space for organic human expression and free exchange of ideas is increasingly being shaped by algorithmic manipulation, commercial interests, and data exploitation. Through the widespread collection of personal data and the use of sophisticated algorithms, these companies have gained unprecedented control over the content users see, the ads they are exposed to, and the behaviors they exhibit online. This has created a curated, commercialized version of the internet that prioritizes profit over privacy and organic human expression. As the digital landscape continues to evolve, it is crucial to consider the implications of data harvesting and the loss of privacy on the freedom of the internet. Only through comprehensive regulation and increased transparency can we ensure that the internet remains a space for authentic, independent voices and free expression.

THE DECLINE OF USER-GENERATED CONTENT: THE SHIFT FROM INDEPENDENT FORUMS, BLOGS, AND WEBSITES TO CENTRALIZED PLATFORMS CONTROLLED BY MAJOR CORPORATIONS

The internet was initially envisioned as a decentralized space for free expression, creativity, and community-building, where individuals could share their thoughts, ideas, and creations with the world. In the early days of the web, independent forums, personal blogs, and niche websites were the primary means through which users generated content, interacted with others, and contributed to the digital landscape. These platforms were open, accessible, and largely free from corporate control. Over the past two decades, however, there has been a significant shift from these independent spaces to centralized platforms controlled by a few large corporations such as Google, Facebook (Meta), Twitter, and Instagram. This transition has had profound implications for the nature of user-generated content, leading to the decline of independent voices, the rise of corporate-driven content, and the commercialization of the internet.

The Rise of Independent Forums, Blogs, and Websites

In the 1990s and early 2000s, the internet was a vast and often chaotic space that allowed individuals to build their own digital worlds. Independent forums, personal blogs, and small, user-run websites were integral to this early internet. These platforms allowed anyone with an internet connection to create and share content, from written articles and videos to artwork, music, and code. At the heart of this early web was a spirit of individuality and decentralization. Platforms like LiveJournal, GeoCities, and early forms of WordPress empowered users to create personal spaces on the internet where they could write freely, share ideas, or connect with like-minded individuals. Independent forums such as Reddit and 4chan were also built around user-generated content, with minimal corporate oversight, enabling diverse communities to form around niche interests and topics.

These early platforms allowed users to be more than just consumers of content—they were creators and contributors, and their input helped shape the culture of the internet. Unlike today's centralized social media platforms, where content is curated by algorithms and driven by corporate interests, the independent websites and blogs of the early internet were a direct reflection of individual creativity, passion, and expertise. The internet was seen as a place where independent voices could thrive, build communities, and engage in the free exchange of ideas.

The Shift to Centralized Platforms

Over time, however, the landscape of the internet began to change. The promise of the web as a decentralized space for free expression started to erode with the rise of large, centralized platforms. As the internet became more commercialized, companies like Google, Facebook, Twitter, YouTube, and Instagram emerged as dominant forces in shaping online culture and content. These platforms quickly gained enormous user bases by offering free services in exchange for user data and content.

Centralized platforms allowed for greater scalability and ease of use. Unlike independent blogs and websites, which required users to manage their own servers and web hosting, platforms like Facebook and Twitter offered user-friendly interfaces that made it easy for anyone to create an account, post content, and interact with others. This accessibility led to the rapid growth of these platforms, which quickly became the primary means by which people interacted with the internet. However, this convenience came with a cost—the shift to centralized platforms also meant that a small number of corporations began to control much of the digital infrastructure and online experiences.

One of the most significant changes brought about by the shift to centralized platforms was the decline of true user-generated content. As major tech companies began to control the platforms, they also started to implement strict guidelines and algorithms that shaped the content that appeared on their sites. For example, platforms like Facebook and Instagram began to prioritize posts and content that would maximize user engagement, often at the expense of organic or independent voices. As algorithms began to drive content visibility, the diversity of voices, topics, and opinions dwindled, with popular posts from individuals or brands gaining far more visibility than content from independent or niche creators.

The Rise of Corporate-Controlled Content

The transition to centralized platforms has also led to the rise of corporate-controlled content. Large corporations, including media companies, influencers, and advertisers, now dominate the digital landscape. These entities use social media platforms and search engines to drive traffic to their products, services, and content, often eclipsing the content created by individual users. The algorithms that power platforms like Facebook, YouTube, and Instagram are designed to favor content that generates high levels of engagement—typically sensational, viral, or commercial content. As a result, user-generated content is increasingly marginalized in favor of content that can drive profits.

The emphasis on engagement-driven content has led to the professionalization of content creation, where the focus shifts from organic, personal expression to content that is optimized for likes, shares, and views. Influencers, brands, and media outlets now dominate much of the content people consume on platforms like Instagram, TikTok, and YouTube. This has created a landscape in which individuals are encouraged to create content that is more polished and commercial, with the goal of gaining followers, monetizing their presence, or promoting products.

This shift is also evident in the way that traditional media outlets have co-opted social media platforms to distribute their content. News organizations, for instance, increasingly rely on platforms like Twitter and Facebook to reach their audiences, resulting in the prioritization of mainstream media narratives over the independent voices that once flourished in digital spaces. The ease with which these platforms allow large organizations to gain exposure has further diminished the visibility of smaller, independent content creators.

The Decline of Personal Blogs and Independent Websites

In addition to the rise of corporate-driven content, the decline of personal blogs and independent websites is another significant consequence of the shift to centralized platforms. Blogs and independent websites once provided a vital space for individuals to express their thoughts, share expertise, and engage with niche communities. However, the dominance of social media and centralized platforms has made it increasingly difficult for personal blogs and websites to attract attention.

The growing prevalence of social media platforms has created an environment where users now spend most of their time interacting with content on Facebook, Instagram, and Twitter, rather than visiting individual websites. As a result, blogs and personal websites, which once represented a vital form of independent expression, have largely been relegated to the margins of the digital world. The monetization of blogs through advertising has also become increasingly difficult, as tech giants like Google and Facebook control much of the advertising market, leaving small-scale bloggers with limited options for generating revenue.

Moreover, the centralized nature of social media platforms has shifted the focus from individuality and independent expression to corporate-driven content. With the rise of algorithms that favor certain types of content, the chances of an independent blog or personal website gaining significant traffic have dwindled. Instead, users are now more likely to encounter content that has been optimized for search engine rankings or tailored to fit the preferences of corporate advertisers.

The Impact on Free Expression and the Organic Internet

The shift from independent forums, blogs, and websites to centralized platforms controlled by major corporations has significant implications for free expression on the internet. In the past, the internet was a space where anyone could create and share content, no matter their background or resources. Today, however, the internet is increasingly commercialized and controlled by a few large companies that prioritize profits over user autonomy and free expression. This has created a digital ecosystem where independent voices struggle to be heard, and the diversity of ideas and content is diminished.

One of the most significant consequences of this shift is the decline of true user-generated content. Platforms like Facebook, Instagram, and Twitter encourage content that adheres to their algorithms, prioritizing posts that maximize user engagement and profit. This leads to the marginalization of organic, independent voices in favor of commercialized content. As a result, the internet has become less of a free space for creative expression and more of a marketplace dominated by a handful of large corporations.

Considerations

The decline of user-generated content, as a result of the shift from independent forums, blogs, and websites to centralized platforms controlled by major corporations, represents a profound transformation in the digital landscape. The internet, once a space for free expression and decentralized interaction, has increasingly become a commercialized ecosystem where corporate interests and algorithms shape the content that users see. This shift has led to the marginalization of independent creators and voices, while the dominance of corporate-controlled content has diminished the diversity of ideas and experiences that once characterized the internet. As the digital world continues to evolve, it is crucial to recognize the impact of this shift on the nature of user-generated content and the erosion of the free, open internet that was once envisioned.

THE DECLINE OF USER-GENERATED CONTENT: THE PRESSURE FOR COMMERCIALIZATION AND ALGORITHMIC CONTENT OVER ORGANIC POSTS

The internet has undergone a significant transformation over the past two decades, transitioning from an open, decentralized space for free expression and individual creativity to a highly commercialized environment dominated by a few large corporations. One of the most prominent changes has been the decline of user-generated content (UGC) in favor of algorithmically curated posts designed to maximize profits and engagement. Platforms that were once celebrated for empowering individuals to share their ideas and build communities are increasingly prioritizing content that drives commercial success, reducing the visibility of organic posts created by independent users. The commercialization of the internet has led to algorithmic systems that prioritize engagement, advertisement-driven content, and viral trends, resulting in the marginalization of authentic, personal expression. This essay explores how the increasing pressure for profits and engagement on digital platforms has led to the decline of user-generated content, and how algorithms have become central to shaping the content users encounter online.

The Rise of User-Generated Content and the Promise of Organic Expression

In the early days of the internet, user-generated content (UGC) was the backbone of many digital spaces. Platforms like personal blogs, forums, and early social media sites such as MySpace and Friendster were places where individuals could create and share content without needing to answer to corporations. Content was raw, authentic, and driven by individuals' personal interests or passions. In these spaces, users engaged with one another organically, sharing thoughts, hobbies, opinions, and ideas in a less curated and more authentic environment.

The power of UGC was in its ability to democratize content creation, allowing anyone with an internet connection to contribute their voice to the digital conversation. Independent bloggers, hobbyists, and small community leaders could thrive by creating content that resonated with specific audiences. Websites like LiveJournal, Blogger, and WordPress allowed users to express themselves freely without the need to optimize for likes, views, or shares. The lack of a profit motive or engagement-centric algorithms created a space where users could publish content that was meaningful, personal, and original.

However, the rise of platforms like Facebook, Twitter, Instagram, and YouTube marked a shift toward centralized, commercialized digital spaces. While these platforms initially allowed users to share content freely, the commercial pressures to drive revenue, engagement, and user retention gradually began to influence the structure of the internet itself.

The Commercialization of Digital Platforms and the Rise of Algorithmic Content

The emergence of major tech companies like Google, Facebook, and Twitter transformed the internet into a profit-driven ecosystem. Social media platforms, in particular, evolved from being simple communication tools to highly commercialized environments that capitalized on user data, advertising, and engagement. These companies generated substantial revenue by using complex algorithms to curate content, serve targeted ads, and keep users engaged for as long as possible.

At the heart of these platforms' business models is the engagement-driven algorithm, which determines what content users see in their feeds. This algorithm is designed to maximize engagement by prioritizing content that is more likely to be shared, liked, commented on, or viewed for an extended period. The content that gets the most engagement is often sensational, emotionally charged, or designed to be easily consumable—characteristics that are more likely to grab attention and go viral. As a result, these algorithms began to prioritize content from influencers, brands, and media outlets—entities that have the resources to produce high-quality, attention-grabbing posts that generate the desired metrics.

While algorithms are responsible for boosting certain types of content, they also create an environment where organic, personal, or niche posts become less visible. Small creators or independent voices often struggle to gain visibility in a landscape where the content that garners the most engagement—usually from professional creators or brands—dominates users' feeds. This leads to a scenario where the algorithms heavily favor commercial content, with personal and original user-generated content pushed to the sidelines. As a result, the internet becomes less of a platform for diverse voices and more of a marketplace for advertising and engagement.

The Pressure for Profits and the Decline of Organic Content

The shift toward algorithm-driven content can be attributed to the pressure these platforms face to generate profits. Social media companies and search engines rely heavily on advertising revenue, which is directly tied to user engagement. The more time users spend on a platform, the more opportunities there are for ads to be served. Therefore, platforms are incentivized to create an environment where users remain engaged for as long as possible, and where advertisers can target specific demographics based on user behavior.

This emphasis on engagement has significantly impacted the nature of the content shared on these platforms. As platforms seek to optimize engagement and user retention, they have increasingly adopted strategies that prioritize viral, click-worthy content. For example, Facebook's algorithm rewards content that garners likes, shares, and comments, while Instagram focuses on content that keeps users scrolling for longer periods. The result is that personal posts, thoughtful commentary, and original content from everyday users struggle to compete with more polished, commercialized posts designed to elicit a reaction.

In turn, many content creators have been forced to adapt their strategies in order to succeed on these platforms. Independent bloggers, for instance, may have started their platforms with the intention of sharing personal insights or creative work, but in order to survive in the current landscape, they often must prioritize SEO (search engine optimization), keywords, and trending topics over authentic self-expression. For video creators on YouTube, this means producing content that is designed to appeal to a wide audience or conform to the latest viral trend rather than content that reflects their unique voice or passion. This shift in focus leads to a homogenization of content across platforms, as users are encouraged to conform to the algorithm's preferences in order to succeed.

The Rise of Influencers and Corporate-Controlled Content

One of the most notable consequences of algorithmic content prioritization is the rise of influencers and corporate-controlled content. The commercialization of digital platforms has given birth to a new class of content creators: influencers. These individuals or brands have learned to work with the algorithmic systems of platforms like Instagram, YouTube, and TikTok to gain massive followings and monetize their content. Influencers and content creators who can create visually appealing, clickable content are now often the ones that dominate the digital space, overshadowing smaller, independent creators who lack the resources to compete in this environment.

For businesses, influencer marketing has become a key strategy for reaching targeted audiences. Influencers use platforms like Instagram and TikTok to advertise products, services, or experiences, often blurring the lines between content creation and advertising. This type of content is inherently algorithm-friendly—professionally produced, visually engaging, and highly shareable. As a result, corporate-sponsored content often outshines organic, user-generated posts, further pushing independent voices to the margins.

In a similar vein, media companies and large corporations now dominate much of the content on social media platforms. As traditional media outlets struggle to maintain relevance in the digital age, they have turned to platforms like Facebook and Twitter to distribute their articles, videos, and news. These corporations, armed with substantial marketing budgets, have learned to create content that resonates with users in a way that maximizes engagement. In turn, this content is amplified by algorithms that prioritize high-traffic stories and viral news. As a result, independent bloggers and small-time content creators have to compete with the power of big corporations to reach a significant audience.

The Erosion of Organic Content Creation

As a result of these commercial pressures, the internet is increasingly dominated by algorithm-driven, commercialized content that is designed to maximize engagement and profit. The once-thriving world of independent, organic user-generated content is increasingly marginalized, as creators are incentivized to tailor their posts to the whims of algorithms rather than produce authentic work. This erosion of organic content has a profound effect on the internet as a space for free expression and creativity. What was once a platform where anyone could share their voice and be heard is now a commercialized marketplace where users must compete for attention within a system designed to prioritize profit over authenticity.

The prioritization of algorithmic content has also led to a more homogenized digital experience. With platforms like Facebook, Instagram, and YouTube placing a premium on viral content and engagement, users are often exposed to the same types of content over and over again. This repetition limits the diversity of ideas, experiences, and perspectives that users are exposed to, reducing the richness of the internet as a medium for free expression.

Considerations

The shift from organic, user-generated content to algorithmically curated content on social media and digital platforms marks a fundamental change in the nature of the internet. As commercialization pressures for engagement and profit have intensified, platforms have increasingly prioritized content that generates high levels of interaction—content that is often driven by influencers, brands, and media outlets. In doing so, they have marginalized independent, personal expression, leading to the decline of authentic user-generated content. This trend has profound implications for the digital landscape, reducing the diversity of voices and experiences and turning the internet into a commercialized marketplace where users are incentivized to create content that adheres to corporate interests rather than organic self-expression. The rise of algorithms and commercial pressures has fundamentally reshaped the internet, leading to the erosion of the free, open space that once allowed users to express themselves without constraint.

THE DECLINE OF USER-GENERATED CONTENT: HOW CLICKBAIT, PAID CONTENT, AND ALGORITHM-DRIVEN ENGAGEMENT RESULT IN A MORE UNIFORM, LESS DIVERSE DIGITAL ECOSYSTEM

The internet has evolved from a platform for personal expression and independent voices into a commercialized ecosystem dominated by algorithm-driven engagement, clickbait headlines, and paid content. One of the most significant changes in recent years has been the decline of authentic, user-generated content (UGC) in favor of content that is optimized for engagement, views, and advertisement-driven revenue. Platforms like Facebook, Instagram, YouTube, and Twitter, once celebrated for their ability to democratize content creation, now prioritize content that maximizes clicks, shares, and likes. This shift has contributed to a more uniform digital ecosystem, where a few types of content dominate the conversation, and the diversity of ideas and voices is increasingly limited. This essay will explore how the rise of clickbait, paid content, and algorithmic manipulation has led to the decline of user-generated content and the reduction of diversity in the digital landscape.

The Rise of Clickbait: Prioritizing Engagement Over Authenticity

In the early days of the internet, much of the content was driven by individual users sharing personal thoughts, experiences, and creative work. Blogs, personal websites, and independent forums were common spaces for users to post organic content that reflected their unique perspectives. However, as the internet matured and monetization became a central focus for many platforms, the pressure to generate more clicks and views led to the rise of clickbait.

Clickbait refers to content that uses sensationalized headlines or provocative images to attract attention, often with little regard for the substance of the content itself. The goal of clickbait is to generate clicks, increase engagement, and, ultimately, boost advertising revenue. As social media platforms became more dependent on user interaction and engagement, the algorithms that power these sites began to prioritize content that elicits strong reactions—content that gets likes, shares, and comments. This results in the amplification of clickbait-driven content, which often sacrifices depth, nuance, and authenticity in favor of quick, viral reactions.

The rise of clickbait has had significant consequences for the digital ecosystem. First, it has led to the proliferation of content that lacks substance, as the primary goal becomes capturing the audience's attention, rather than providing meaningful information or fostering in-depth discussions. This content is often designed to appeal to emotions—fear, anger, surprise, or curiosity—rather than intellect or thoughtful exploration. While clickbait content may garner more immediate engagement, it ultimately contributes to a homogenization of the types of content that dominate users' feeds, further reducing the diversity of voices and perspectives online.

Paid Content: How Advertisers Shape What We See

In addition to the rise of clickbait, paid content has become a dominant force in shaping the digital landscape. Paid content refers to advertisements or sponsored posts that appear in users' feeds, often designed to blend seamlessly with organic content. With the rise of social media platforms and the growth of digital advertising, these platforms have increasingly relied on paid content as a major revenue stream.

Social media sites, search engines, and even video platforms like YouTube have incorporated paid content into their algorithms, often promoting ads and sponsored posts alongside organic user-generated content. In some cases, users may not even recognize that the content they are engaging with is paid for, as these sponsored posts are often tailored to match the tone, style, and format of user-generated posts. The seamless integration of ads into content feeds makes it harder for users to distinguish between genuine, organic posts and content created for commercial purposes.

Paid content has further contributed to the decline of authentic user-generated content because it favors advertisers and large corporations that can afford to pay for visibility. Independent content creators, hobbyists, and small businesses often struggle to compete with the volume and sophistication of paid ads. As a result, paid content often receives more visibility and engagement than organic content, further pushing smaller voices to the margins of the digital ecosystem.

Moreover, paid content and advertisements are often tailored to exploit user preferences, creating an environment where content is algorithmically manipulated to match the user's previous behaviors, interests, and buying habits. This results in a more personalized, but less diverse, experience. Instead of encountering a broad range of perspectives or new ideas, users are exposed to a narrowed view of the digital world, where the majority of content is designed to sell something or reinforce existing preferences.

Algorithm-Driven Engagement: The Homogenization of Online Content

The most significant driver of the decline in user-generated content and the increased uniformity of the digital ecosystem is the rise of algorithm-driven engagement. Social media platforms and search engines use sophisticated algorithms to determine what content appears in users' feeds, search results, and recommendations. These algorithms prioritize content that is likely to generate the most engagement—content that gets clicked, liked, shared, or commented on. However, this reliance on engagement metrics to determine visibility has created a system where content is often sensationalized, superficial, or optimized for virality rather than authenticity or originality.

Platforms like Facebook, Twitter, Instagram, and YouTube have developed algorithms that push content designed to grab attention quickly. As a result, posts that are engaging on an emotional level—whether positive or negative—are more likely to appear in users' feeds. This prioritization of engagement leads to a situation where more thoughtful or nuanced content often gets buried beneath viral posts or clickbait-driven media. Instead of fostering a rich and diverse environment for content creation, the algorithmic system rewards content that conforms to certain patterns, reducing the variety of voices and ideas that users encounter.

The algorithmic focus on engagement has also made it more difficult for independent content creators to gain visibility without adhering to the rules of engagement. Content creators must now learn to optimize their posts for the algorithm, often creating posts that are designed to generate high levels of interaction, rather than those that reflect their unique perspective. This can result in a form of self-censorship, as creators may feel compelled to create content that is more sensational or more likely to go viral, rather than content that might be more reflective of their personal experiences or authentic voices.

Additionally, algorithmic manipulation fosters a cycle of homogeneity, where users are consistently exposed to similar types of content. Algorithms determine what content to show based on user preferences and past interactions, creating filter bubbles that limit the diversity of information and ideas. Users are less likely to encounter content that challenges their beliefs or exposes them to new viewpoints. Instead, they are shown content that reinforces existing ideas, leading to a more uniform and less diverse digital ecosystem.

The Impact on the Diversity of Voices and Ideas

The rise of clickbait, paid content, and algorithm-driven engagement has led to a reduction in the diversity of voices and ideas that are represented online. As platforms prioritize content that maximizes engagement and generates revenue, the internet has become less of an open space for free expression and more of a commercialized marketplace. The pressure to optimize for clicks, views, and shares has resulted in the rise of content that conforms to a narrow set of parameters, rather than content that reflects the full spectrum of human experience.

Independent voices, niche communities, and small creators who once thrived on the internet are increasingly marginalized in favor of content that is designed to appeal to the broadest possible audience. These creators struggle to compete with the vast resources of large corporations, media outlets, and influencers who can afford to create content that is tailored to the algorithms of major platforms. As a result, the diversity of ideas, experiences, and perspectives is diminished, and the digital ecosystem becomes more homogenous, favoring mainstream, sensationalized, and commercially-driven content.

Moreover, the focus on engagement-driven content has made the internet a space where entertainment and profit take precedence over authenticity, knowledge, or genuine connection. Instead of using digital platforms to express individuality or share personal insights, users are often incentivized to produce content that fits into predefined molds, optimized for clicks and viral success. This shift undermines the creative freedom that once defined the internet, turning it into a platform for commercial gain rather than a space for free and organic self-expression.

Considerations

The rise of clickbait, paid content, and algorithm-driven engagement has significantly impacted the digital ecosystem, leading to the decline of user-generated content and the creation of a more uniform, less diverse online space. While algorithms and monetization strategies have allowed platforms to generate substantial revenue, they have also resulted in the marginalization of independent voices, the homogenization of content, and the prioritization of viral, click-worthy material over authenticity and originality. The internet, once a dynamic space for free expression, is now dominated by content that is designed to maximize engagement and profit, reducing the diversity of ideas and perspectives that once characterized the digital world. As the commercialization of the internet continues to shape the content users encounter, it is important to recognize the implications this shift has for the future of user-generated content and the overall health of the digital ecosystem.

THE ROLE OF GOVERNMENT AND CORPORATIONS IN SHAPING THE INTERNET: SURVEILLANCE AND CONTROL

The internet has revolutionized communication, commerce, and culture, providing users with unprecedented access to information and opportunities for global interaction. However, as the internet has evolved, so too have concerns about its control and regulation. Governments and corporations have increasingly sought to monitor, shape, and control online activity, often in ways that can stifle free speech and diminish the authentic nature of internet interactions. This essay explores the role of government agencies and corporate interests in the surveillance and control of internet activity, examining how such actions can undermine personal freedoms, inhibit genuine interaction, and erode privacy.

Government Surveillance: The Expansion of Control and Monitoring

Governments around the world have long been interested in the internet as a tool for surveillance and control. In many cases, governments have justified their surveillance programs as necessary for national security, crime prevention, and counterterrorism efforts. However, the increasing sophistication and reach of government surveillance programs have raised significant concerns about the balance between security and individual rights, particularly in terms of privacy and freedom of expression.

One of the most notable instances of government surveillance on the internet occurred in 2013, when former NSA contractor Edward Snowden revealed the extent of the United States National Security Agency's (NSA) surveillance programs.

These programs, including the mass collection of phone metadata and online communications through programs like PRISM, demonstrated the ability of governments to monitor the online activities of millions of citizens, both domestically and abroad. This surveillance extended to email, chat services, social media, and internet browsing history, without the need for individual warrants or specific legal justification.

The revelations about government surveillance programs sparked widespread concern about the erosion of privacy rights and the chilling effect such monitoring can have on free speech. When individuals know they are being watched, they are less likely to express themselves freely or engage in open discussions, fearing retribution or surveillance. This phenomenon, often referred to as the "chilling effect," stifles genuine internet interactions and can discourage users from participating in online discussions or sharing personal opinions. The fear of government surveillance, particularly among activists, journalists, and political dissenters, raises serious questions about the extent to which governments can justify their intrusion into the digital lives of citizens in the name of security.

Moreover, government surveillance programs are often opaque, with citizens having little knowledge of the extent to which they are being monitored or the specific data being collected. This lack of transparency undermines the trust that users place in digital platforms and can result in a more passive, self-censoring internet environment. As users become more aware of the government's ability to track their every online move, they may become less likely to engage in meaningful, open interactions, reducing the authenticity of the online experience.

Corporate Interests and Data Harvesting: The Privatization of Surveillance

While government surveillance is a well-known issue, corporate interests in internet monitoring and control are also significant and increasingly pervasive. Corporations, particularly tech giants like Google, Facebook, Amazon, and Microsoft, have enormous influence over how the internet functions, and their role in shaping online behavior has far-reaching implications for privacy, freedom of speech, and access to information.

The central business model of many large tech companies is based on data harvesting and targeted advertising. Platforms like Facebook, Instagram, Google, and YouTube collect vast amounts of personal data from users, including browsing history, location data, preferences, social interactions, and even facial recognition data. This data is used to build detailed profiles of users that can be sold to advertisers or used to serve targeted advertisements, making these platforms highly profitable. However, this business model has raised significant concerns about privacy violations and the extent to which corporate interests control the flow of information on the internet.

The data collected by these corporations often includes sensitive information, such as political preferences, health issues, or personal beliefs, making users vulnerable to exploitation and manipulation. For example, the Cambridge Analytica scandal in 2018 exposed how Facebook allowed third-party companies to access the personal data of millions of users without their consent. This data was then used to create psychological profiles of users, which were exploited in political campaigns. The incident highlighted the ways in which corporations can manipulate user data to influence behavior, potentially distorting democratic processes and restricting access to objective, unbiased information.

Furthermore, the control that corporations have over the content users see online also contributes to surveillance and control. Social media platforms, search engines, and video sharing sites increasingly rely on algorithms to determine what content is shown to users. These algorithms are designed to prioritize content that will generate the most engagement, typically based on user preferences and past behaviors. This control over content curation can limit the diversity of information that users encounter and create filter bubbles, where users are exposed primarily to content that reinforces their existing views.

In some cases, corporations have also engaged in self-censorship in response to government pressures or to avoid controversy. Social media platforms like Twitter, Facebook, and YouTube have faced increasing pressure to regulate content, remove harmful posts, and combat "fake news." While these efforts are often presented as a way to protect users from misinformation and harmful content, they also raise concerns about corporate censorship and the restriction of free speech. Corporate interests, in combination with government regulations, can lead to the creation of an internet that is heavily curated and controlled, potentially stifling authentic interaction and the free exchange of ideas.

The Impact on Free Speech and Internet Freedom

The combination of government surveillance and corporate data harvesting creates a digital environment where users are constantly being monitored, influenced, and controlled. The primary concern is that this level of surveillance undermines the principles of free speech and privacy that the internet was originally designed to protect.

Government and corporate surveillance, whether conducted overtly or covertly, creates a system where individuals are no longer free to express their opinions and engage in meaningful dialogue without fear of reprisal or manipulation. The more data that is collected, the more power corporations and governments have to shape what individuals see, think, and do online. This power can lead to a narrowing of discourse, as users are subjected to highly targeted content that aligns with corporate or governmental agendas, rather than being exposed to a wide range of diverse, independent viewpoints.

Furthermore, the chilling effect caused by surveillance can lead to a decline in the quality of online discussions. If users fear that their online activities are being tracked, they may avoid engaging in sensitive or controversial conversations. In some cases, individuals may censor themselves or adopt false identities to protect their privacy, ultimately undermining the authenticity of online interactions. This self-censorship can contribute to the decline of an open, democratic internet, where people are free to express themselves without fear of surveillance, retribution, or manipulation.

The issue of free speech extends beyond individual users to the broader societal implications of control over digital platforms. When a few large corporations control access to information, it raises questions about who has the power to shape public discourse and influence societal norms. The centralized nature of the internet means that a small group of tech giants can have a disproportionate influence over what information is accessible and what is not, limiting the diversity of ideas and voices.

The Need for Accountability and Transparency

The role of government agencies and corporations in shaping the internet through surveillance and control raises critical concerns about privacy, free speech, and the authenticity of online interactions. Government surveillance programs, justified by national security concerns, can erode privacy and create a chilling effect on free expression. At the same time, corporate interests in data harvesting and content manipulation contribute to the commercialization of the internet, often at the expense of diversity and independent voices.

To preserve the integrity of the internet as a space for open communication and personal expression, it is essential that both governments and corporations be held accountable for their surveillance practices. Transparency in how personal data is collected and used, as well as clear policies regarding content moderation, are crucial steps toward ensuring that the internet remains a platform for genuine interaction and free speech. In a world where control over the digital landscape is increasingly concentrated in the hands of a few powerful entities, safeguarding the principles of privacy, freedom of expression, and diversity of thought must be a priority. Only then can we protect the internet as a space for open dialogue and democratic engagement.

STATE-SPONSORED CENSORSHIP AND DISINFORMATION: SHAPING AN ARTIFICIAL INTERNET

The internet, which was once lauded as a democratizing force capable of giving voice to the voiceless, has increasingly become a battleground for competing interests—governments, corporations, and political factions—seeking to influence and control the flow of information. While governments and corporations have long been involved in regulating online content, there is growing concern about state-sponsored censorship and disinformation campaigns that intentionally suppress certain narratives while promoting others. This deliberate manipulation of information creates a more artificial version of the internet, one in which the free exchange of ideas is undermined by political, corporate, and state interests. This essay will explore how state-sponsored censorship and disinformation are contributing to the creation of an artificial internet and the implications of this trend for free speech, democracy, and the future of digital engagement.

State-Sponsored Censorship: Suppressing Dissenting Voices

State-sponsored censorship refers to the practice of governments directly controlling, restricting, or influencing the content that is available online. This form of censorship is often implemented under the guise of protecting national security, public order, or social stability. However, the impact of state-sponsored censorship is much broader, often curbing free speech, stifling dissent, and suppressing unpopular or politically inconvenient viewpoints.

In many authoritarian regimes, state-sponsored censorship is an essential tool for maintaining control over the population. Governments routinely block access to websites that promote opposition views, critical journalism, or independent thought. For example, in countries like China and Russia, governments have implemented extensive censorship measures, including the blocking of social media platforms, news outlets, and other online resources that criticize the regime. In China, the "Great Firewall" is a sophisticated system of internet filtering that prevents citizens from accessing foreign news, social media sites like Facebook and Twitter, and other content deemed harmful to the state's ideological interests. Similarly, Russia has passed laws requiring internet service providers to block access to content that criticizes the government or spreads what it considers "extremist" ideas.

Even in more democratic societies, state-sponsored censorship is becoming an increasing concern. Governments may not block access to websites outright but engage in more subtle forms of control, such as pressuring social media platforms to remove certain types of content. The 2020 U.S. presidential election, for instance, saw government agencies and political leaders calling for the removal of disinformation, which led to content moderation practices by platforms like Facebook, Twitter, and YouTube. While this was presented as a means of protecting the public from falsehoods, it also raised questions about the limits of free speech and the potential for the government to exert too much influence over what citizens are allowed to read, discuss, and share online.

State-sponsored censorship can also manifest in the form of "content localization" policies. These policies often require that online content comply with national laws and regulations. For instance, Germany has passed laws that mandate the removal of hate speech from social media platforms within 24 hours. While such laws may be intended to address harmful content, they can also be used to suppress dissent or limit the scope of political debate. When governments control what information is accessible, they effectively limit the ability of individuals to form independent opinions and make informed decisions.

The impact of state-sponsored censorship is far-reaching. It distorts the free flow of information, inhibits democratic debate, and forces citizens to rely on state-approved narratives. In the absence of diverse viewpoints and critical voices, the internet becomes a less open and less trustworthy space for public discourse.

Disinformation Campaigns: Manipulating Narratives and Undermining Trust

In addition to state-sponsored censorship, many governments and political entities have been accused of using disinformation campaigns to push particular narratives and influence public opinion. Disinformation, the deliberate spreading of false or misleading information, is a powerful tool for governments and corporations to control the narrative and manipulate public perception. Unlike misinformation, which may be the result of ignorance or error, disinformation is intentionally crafted to deceive.

State-sponsored disinformation campaigns often focus on shaping public attitudes about key political issues, discrediting opposition leaders, or manipulating elections. These campaigns are not limited to authoritarian regimes but are increasingly common in democratic societies as well. For example, Russia has been accused of orchestrating disinformation campaigns during the 2016 U.S. presidential election, using social media platforms to sow division, spread false narratives, and manipulate voters. The Internet Research Agency (IRA), a Russian government-linked entity, created fake social media accounts to disseminate divisive content and promote pro-Russian messages. Similarly, in other countries, governments have employed social media bots and fake accounts to spread disinformation, with the goal of swaying public opinion or influencing political outcomes.

The tactics used in disinformation campaigns are diverse and sophisticated. They often involve the use of bots—automated accounts that generate and spread content at a rapid pace. These bots can amplify particular messages, create the illusion of widespread support, and sway public sentiment. Social media platforms are particularly vulnerable to these campaigns because of their reliance on algorithms that prioritize sensational or engaging content. Disinformation can go viral quickly, especially if it taps into pre-existing political or social tensions.

Beyond election manipulation, state-sponsored disinformation campaigns also target sensitive social issues, such as public health, climate change, and international relations. The spread of misinformation about COVID-19, for example, has been attributed to both state and non-state actors attempting to promote certain political agendas or undermine public trust in scientific institutions. The proliferation of conspiracy theories and false information about vaccines, for instance, has been fueled by coordinated disinformation campaigns that exploit online platforms to spread distrust and confusion.

The effect of disinformation on society is profound. It erodes trust in democratic institutions, media outlets, and even scientific research. As people become exposed to false narratives, they may lose confidence in the truth and become more susceptible to believing fabricated or manipulated information. Disinformation campaigns not only distort public opinion but also diminish the credibility of the internet as a source of reliable information.

The Creation of an Artificial Internet: Suppressing Diversity of Thought

Together, state-sponsored censorship and disinformation campaigns contribute to the creation of an artificial internet, one where the flow of information is manipulated and controlled by powerful political and corporate forces. Rather than serving as a platform for the free exchange of ideas, the internet becomes a battleground for competing narratives, often shaped by those with the most resources and political power.

The suppression of dissenting voices and the amplification of certain narratives creates a digital environment where diversity of thought is stifled. Individuals are exposed to a limited range of viewpoints and are often steered toward content that aligns with the interests of governments or corporations. Algorithms that prioritize engagement, coupled with government influence over social media platforms, create a filter bubble effect where users are rarely exposed to alternative perspectives or challenging ideas. As a result, the internet becomes less of an open forum and more of a controlled, curated space that serves the interests of a select few.

This artificial version of the internet has profound implications for democracy and free expression. When governments and corporations control the information that people receive, they effectively shape the public's understanding of reality. Citizens may struggle to make informed decisions if the information they rely on is biased, manipulated, or incomplete. Furthermore, when people cannot freely discuss political issues, voice criticism, or share alternative viewpoints, the democratic process is undermined.

Safeguarding the Integrity of the Internet

The increasing role of governments and corporations in shaping the internet through censorship and disinformation campaigns poses a serious threat to the authenticity and openness of online spaces. The deliberate suppression of dissent and the manipulation of public opinion create an artificial digital environment where freedom of expression and democratic debate are undermined. To preserve the integrity of the internet, it is crucial that both governments and corporations be held accountable for their role in shaping online content. Transparency, accountability, and robust protections for free speech are essential to ensuring that the internet remains a platform for genuine interaction, the free exchange of ideas, and informed democratic participation. Without these safeguards, the internet risks becoming a controlled space, subject to manipulation by powerful actors seeking to shape the narratives that define our reality.

THE PSYCHOLOGICAL AND SOCIAL IMPLICATIONS OF THE EROSION OF TRUST IN INFORMATION

The internet, once seen as a democratizing force providing unprecedented access to information, has become increasingly fragmented and unreliable. As artificial intelligence (AI), bots, and misinformation proliferate online, users are increasingly finding it difficult to trust the content they encounter. This erosion of trust in online information has significant psychological and social implications. People are experiencing heightened skepticism, confusion, and anxiety about the reliability of information, which can have profound effects on decision-making, social relationships, and the overall functioning of democratic societies. This essay explores the psychological and social consequences of diminished trust in online content, focusing on the mental health risks, the spread of misinformation, and the weakening of social cohesion.

Psychological Impacts: Anxiety, Cognitive Dissonance, and Information Overload

One of the most immediate psychological effects of the erosion of trust in online information is heightened anxiety. As people encounter a growing volume of content generated by AI, bots, and malicious actors, they may feel overwhelmed by the uncertainty of whether the information they are consuming is accurate or trustworthy. This cognitive dissonance—holding conflicting beliefs about the reliability of information—can create a sense of unease, as users struggle to navigate an increasingly complex digital landscape. Research shows that the constant exposure to contradictory or misleading content can cause feelings of confusion, frustration, and stress, which in turn erodes individuals' confidence in their ability to discern truth from falsehood.

In an environment where truth seems elusive, people may experience "information fatigue," characterized by feelings of being overwhelmed by the sheer volume of information they are expected to process daily. This constant barrage of content, much of which may be fabricated or distorted, leads to mental exhaustion and cognitive overload. The brain's capacity to process information effectively becomes strained, and as a result, individuals may begin to disengage from critical thinking or become overly reliant on superficial cues—such as headlines, endorsements, or social media likes—rather than carefully evaluating the accuracy and credibility of the information. Over time, this tendency can erode critical thinking skills and promote passive consumption of media, making individuals more susceptible to manipulation by biased or deceptive content.

The trust deficit also contributes to increased skepticism. Individuals may begin to question not only the credibility of online content but also their ability to judge the validity of information. This erosion of confidence can foster a sense of helplessness, where users feel that it is no longer possible to separate fact from fiction in an increasingly AI-driven digital ecosystem. Cognitive biases—such as confirmation bias—can exacerbate this situation, as people seek out information that aligns with their pre-existing beliefs, further reinforcing misinformation and polarizing individuals within echo chambers.

The Spread of Misinformation: Fragmenting Public Discourse

The proliferation of misinformation, driven by bots, AI-generated content, and coordinated disinformation campaigns, is another critical consequence of the erosion of trust in information. Online platforms—particularly social media—serve as fertile ground for misinformation to spread rapidly, fueled by algorithmic amplification. These platforms prioritize engagement, meaning that sensational, controversial, or emotionally charged content tends to be pushed to the forefront, regardless of its veracity. As misinformation is often designed to exploit emotional responses, it has a much higher chance of going viral than factual, nuanced content.

This creates a fragmented information landscape where truth becomes increasingly difficult to discern. Users are bombarded with conflicting narratives on the same topics, leading to confusion and a lack of consensus on key issues. The consequences of this fragmentation are particularly evident in the realm of politics and public health. For example, during the COVID-19 pandemic, misinformation about the virus, vaccines, and public health measures was widely disseminated through social media platforms, often undermining scientific consensus and causing confusion and fear among the public. The misinformation was sometimes amplified by bots or even state-sponsored actors who had an interest in spreading distrust in public health institutions or sowing division.

The erosion of trust in the content users encounter online has also contributed to the growing phenomenon of "alternative facts" and conspiracy theories. As users become more skeptical of mainstream narratives, they may turn to fringe websites or forums where misinformation is rife. The increasing reliance on alternative, often unverified, sources of information can further polarize societies, as people retreat into insular ideological bubbles that reinforce their beliefs and dismiss contrary viewpoints. This fragmentation of the information ecosystem diminishes the potential for constructive public discourse and undermines the foundation of shared knowledge upon which democratic societies rely.

Social Implications: Polarization, Erosion of Social Trust, and Fragmented Communities

The psychological consequences of misinformation and AI-generated content have far-reaching social implications. As trust in online information declines, so too does trust in the social fabric that holds communities together. Trust is the cornerstone of social cohesion, and without it, societies begin to fracture. When individuals no longer trust the information they encounter online, they are less likely to trust others. This distrust, when compounded by the prevalence of misinformation, can lead to greater social polarization.

In political contexts, misinformation is often used to fuel division and create animosity between different ideological groups. As social media algorithms amplify content that promotes division and outrage, people become increasingly entrenched in their beliefs, often viewing those with opposing viewpoints as threats or enemies. This erosion of social trust can undermine the ability to have productive, respectful conversations about important issues, making it more difficult to find common ground or achieve consensus on key social and political challenges.

The rise of misinformation also makes it more difficult to build and maintain meaningful relationships, both online and offline. When individuals are exposed to distorted or false content, it can foster mistrust in institutions, individuals, and even friends and family members. The spread of fake news and AI-generated content can create a divide between people who believe in competing narratives, making it harder to engage in open dialogue and compromise. This fragmentation is evident in the growing phenomenon of "echo chambers," where individuals only engage with content and people who share their views, reinforcing their existing biases.

Moreover, the inability to trust online content can also have profound implications for civic engagement and democratic participation. When citizens lose confidence in the information they encounter, they may disengage from the political process altogether. Voter apathy, reduced participation in public debates, and diminished confidence in democratic institutions can all be attributed to the erosion of trust in the content that shapes public opinion. In this sense, the erosion of trust in information poses a direct threat to the functioning of democracy itself, as it becomes more difficult for citizens to make informed decisions or participate meaningfully in the political process.

Addressing the Trust Crisis in the Digital Age

The erosion of trust in online information, fueled by the rise of AI-generated content, bots, and misinformation, is having profound psychological and social consequences. Users are experiencing heightened anxiety, cognitive dissonance, and information overload, which can impair their ability to critically assess content. The spread of misinformation, facilitated by algorithmic amplification, is fragmenting public discourse and fostering polarization. On a social level, the decline in trust is eroding social cohesion, making it harder to engage in productive conversations and undermining the foundations of democracy.

To address the psychological and social implications of this trust crisis, it is essential to implement strategies that prioritize transparency, accountability, and media literacy. Platforms must take greater responsibility for the content they host, while governments and civil society must collaborate to ensure that users have the tools and knowledge to critically evaluate the information they encounter. Only by restoring trust in the online ecosystem can we mitigate the negative psychological and social effects of a fragmented, misinformation-filled digital landscape. The future of a well-functioning, democratic society depends on our ability to rebuild trust in the information that shapes our world.

THE PSYCHOLOGICAL AND SOCIAL IMPLICATIONS OF SOCIAL ISOLATION AND ECHO CHAMBERS

The digital age has radically transformed the way people interact, access information, and form opinions. While the internet has facilitated unprecedented global connections, it has also fostered a new form of social isolation: echo chambers. Echo chambers are online environments where individuals are exposed only to information, opinions, and content that reinforce their existing beliefs, leading to a narrowing of perspectives and a decrease in meaningful engagement with diverse viewpoints. This phenomenon is largely driven by algorithmic content, where social media platforms and search engines prioritize content based on user preferences and past behavior. While these algorithms are designed to enhance user engagement, they have unintended consequences, including social isolation, polarization, and a breakdown in social cohesion. This essay explores the psychological and social implications of social isolation and echo chambers, focusing on how algorithm-driven content contributes to the creation of these bubbles, reduces meaningful interaction, and diminishes the diversity of thought.

Social Isolation: The Psychological Impact of Being Surrounded by Like-Minded Views

One of the primary psychological implications of social isolation in digital spaces is the reinforcement of existing beliefs and cognitive biases. The human tendency toward "confirmation bias" — the inclination to seek out information that supports one's pre-existing views — is amplified in an environment where algorithmic systems selectively present content based on past behavior. When users interact with certain types of content, social media platforms use this data to predict and surface similar content, thereby creating a feedback loop that isolates them from opposing perspectives.

While this can provide comfort and validation, it also has negative psychological effects. The constant exposure to like-minded views can lead to a sense of intellectual stagnation, as individuals are not challenged to reconsider or critically assess their own beliefs. This isolation in the digital sphere can lead to a false sense of certainty, where individuals believe their perspective is universally shared and validated by others. Over time, this reinforcement can strengthen emotional attachment to certain ideologies, making it more difficult for individuals to engage with new information or alternative perspectives. As a result, people become more rigid in their thinking, less open to change, and more resistant to the idea that others might have valid, differing opinions.

Moreover, social isolation in echo chambers can contribute to a heightened sense of insecurity, anxiety, and frustration. When individuals are surrounded by homogeneous viewpoints and do not encounter challenging or conflicting opinions, they may develop a distorted perception of reality. If they are exposed to information or arguments that contradict their beliefs, they may perceive these as threats to their identity or worldview, which can generate defensive emotional responses. This anxiety is particularly evident in political or social contexts, where deeply held beliefs can become intertwined with a person's sense of self-worth or group identity. The resulting polarization makes meaningful dialogue difficult and increases the emotional stakes of every debate, making it more likely that individuals will engage in adversarial rather than constructive communication.

Echo Chambers: Narrowing Perspectives and Fostering Polarization

Echo chambers do not only affect the individual but also have far-reaching social consequences. As individuals become increasingly isolated within their own ideological bubbles, society as a whole becomes more fragmented and polarized. The idea of "the other" — those who hold different views — becomes more pronounced, creating an "us vs. them" mentality. This polarization can undermine social trust and erode the sense of community that is vital for functioning democracies and healthy societies.

One of the ways in which echo chambers foster polarization is by encouraging groupthink. In digital spaces where like-minded individuals gather, there is a strong tendency for group members to reinforce one another's views, sometimes to an extreme degree. The desire for social acceptance and approval within the group leads individuals to become more extreme in their positions, as the boundaries of acceptable discourse narrow. This dynamic can drive individuals further away from centrist or moderate positions and push them toward more radical or fringe beliefs. This is particularly problematic when it comes to issues such as politics, public health, or social justice, where extreme viewpoints may be amplified in echo chambers, influencing individuals to reject more balanced or fact-based perspectives.

Social media platforms, in particular, exacerbate this process. Platforms like Facebook, Twitter, and YouTube use algorithms that prioritize content that generates strong emotional reactions — typically content that is sensational, divisive, or polarizing. As users interact with content that aligns with their interests, they are continuously fed similar materials that amplify their views. In the process, they may be unaware of the broader spectrum of opinions on an issue, and their sense of what is "normal" or "acceptable" may become increasingly skewed. This phenomenon is especially evident in political discourse, where the increasing tribalism of online communities can contribute to greater social division.

Algorithmic Content and the Creation of Filter Bubbles

The role of algorithms in the formation of echo chambers cannot be overstated. Algorithms used by social media platforms and content-sharing websites are designed to optimize user engagement by recommending content based on users' previous interactions, preferences, and browsing histories. While this personalization aims to enhance user experience, it also means that users are often exposed to a narrower range of viewpoints and information.

This process is known as the "filter bubble" effect, a term coined by Internet activist Eli Pariser in 2011. Filter bubbles occur when algorithms isolate individuals from content that challenges their views, creating a digital environment where only certain perspectives are visible. Users within a filter bubble may be unaware of alternative viewpoints and are less likely to encounter content that could provide a broader, more nuanced understanding of an issue. This selective exposure to content fosters an environment where individuals are less likely to engage in meaningful dialogue with others who hold differing opinions. The more people engage with content within their bubble, the more their information consumption is refined to match their preferences, creating an increasingly homogeneous online experience.

The result of these filter bubbles is the creation of isolated, self-reinforcing communities that may not engage with the broader societal conversations. The internet, rather than serving as a platform for open and diverse discussion, becomes a fragmented space where users are sheltered from differing viewpoints. In this context, social isolation is not only a personal issue but a societal one, as it reduces opportunities for constructive discourse and mutual understanding. When individuals are not exposed to a range of opinions, they may become less empathetic to others and less willing to compromise, fostering a polarized and divisive society.

Reducing Meaningful Engagement and Diversity of Thought

One of the most concerning consequences of algorithmic content curation is the decline in meaningful engagement and the narrowing of intellectual diversity. Echo chambers and filter bubbles contribute to an online ecosystem where individuals are less likely to encounter diverse perspectives and more likely to engage in shallow interactions that reinforce existing beliefs. This phenomenon undermines the richness of online discourse, which is vital for fostering a healthy public sphere.

Meaningful engagement requires exposure to diverse viewpoints, critical thinking, and respectful debate. When users are only exposed to content that aligns with their pre-existing beliefs, they are less likely to engage deeply with ideas that challenge their worldview. Instead, interactions may become more about affirming one's own beliefs or "winning" an argument, rather than fostering mutual understanding. This shallow form of engagement reduces the quality of discussions and hinders the development of well-rounded, informed opinions.

Furthermore, the narrowing of viewpoints reduces the diversity of thought in online spaces. The internet, which has the potential to connect individuals from diverse backgrounds, becomes instead a space dominated by homogeneous groups with little exposure to alternative perspectives. This lack of diversity limits intellectual creativity and stifles innovation. When everyone thinks in similar ways, the range of solutions to social, political, and economic challenges becomes constrained, making it harder to solve complex global problems.

Rebuilding Engagement and Diversifying Thought

The psychological and social implications of social isolation and echo chambers are profound. The rise of algorithmic content curation has created a digital environment where individuals are increasingly isolated within their own belief systems, leading to polarization, a reduction in meaningful engagement, and a narrowing of intellectual diversity. These developments pose serious challenges to the quality of public discourse, democratic engagement, and social cohesion.

To address these issues, it is important to recognize the role of algorithms in shaping the information ecosystem. Social media platforms, content providers, and users themselves must prioritize exposure to diverse perspectives, critical thinking, and constructive dialogue. By promoting transparency in algorithmic design, encouraging media literacy, and fostering spaces where diverse viewpoints can be heard and respected, we can mitigate the harmful effects of echo chambers and create a more inclusive and vibrant digital landscape. Only by embracing the diversity of thought that the internet has the potential to offer can we ensure that it remains a space for meaningful engagement, growth, and connection.

AI'S IMPACT ON IDENTITY AND RELATIONSHIPS: THE PSYCHOLOGICAL EFFECTS OF INTERACTING WITH BOTS AND AI INSTEAD OF REAL PEOPLE

The rapid development of artificial intelligence (AI) technologies has fundamentally altered how people interact with the world around them. AI has become a ubiquitous part of daily life, from virtual assistants like Siri and Alexa to chatbots on social media platforms and in customer service roles. While these advancements have brought many benefits, including increased convenience and efficiency, they also have profound psychological implications. The shift from real human interaction to AI-driven exchanges has raised concerns about the effects on identity, social relationships, and overall mental well-being. This essay explores how AI is impacting personal identity and relationships, focusing on the psychological effects of interacting with bots and AI rather than real people, and how these changes could lead to loneliness, social disconnection, and even identity fragmentation.

The Psychological Shift: From Human Interaction to AI Engagement

Humans are inherently social beings, and meaningful social interactions are crucial for psychological well-being. The need for human connection is deeply embedded in our biology and psychology. Human relationships provide essential emotional support, opportunities for empathy, and a sense of belonging. Historically, these needs were met through face-to-face interaction with others in the physical world. However, the rise of AI has introduced a shift toward digital interactions that are mediated by algorithms, often replacing human involvement in many aspects of communication and support.

AI-driven bots and systems are designed to simulate human-like conversations and provide personalized services. Virtual assistants and chatbots have become commonplace in customer service, healthcare, and even social media platforms. While these technologies are efficient and often effective in delivering services, they cannot replicate the nuances of human interaction. They lack true empathy, understanding, and the emotional intelligence that real human connections provide. This presents a fundamental psychological shift: individuals are increasingly engaging with machines that mimic human responses but do not possess the authenticity and emotional depth of real people.

Interacting with bots or AI systems rather than human beings can have a profound impact on a person's sense of identity. Human interactions allow individuals to express themselves, receive validation, and feel understood. When these interactions are replaced by AI, the dynamic shifts. AI, no matter how sophisticated, lacks the capacity for genuine empathy or reciprocal emotional exchange. Over time, this can lead individuals to feel alienated from their own emotions or unsure of how to relate to others, as their social needs are no longer met in a meaningful way. The AI may provide functional responses but lacks the depth of human engagement, which is essential for maintaining a sense of self.

Loneliness and Social Disconnection: AI as a Substitute for Real Relationships

One of the most significant psychological effects of interacting with AI instead of real people is the potential for loneliness. Loneliness is a state of emotional isolation in which individuals feel disconnected from others, even if they are physically surrounded by people. In the digital age, loneliness has become increasingly prevalent, and AI-driven interactions may exacerbate this problem. Although chatbots and virtual assistants can simulate conversation, they do not provide the emotional connection that is essential for reducing loneliness.

AI interactions may give individuals the illusion of connection, but they lack the richness of human relationships. Genuine human relationships are built on shared experiences, emotional exchanges, and mutual understanding. These elements foster trust and connection, which AI cannot replicate. For individuals who interact primarily with AI systems, the resulting emotional disconnection can deepen feelings of isolation. This phenomenon is particularly concerning in the context of younger generations who have grown up with technology and may struggle to form strong, face-to-face social connections.

For example, individuals who frequently engage with AI-driven customer service bots or virtual friends might experience a lack of emotional fulfillment that could lead to social disconnection. The more time spent interacting with AI, the less time is spent developing real relationships with human beings, which can contribute to a growing sense of loneliness. Additionally, AI interactions do not fulfill the emotional need for companionship and social bonding that humans crave. As a result, individuals may find themselves retreating further into virtual spaces, where social isolation is perpetuated rather than alleviated.

The Impact on Relationships: AI as a Substitute for Human Connection

AI's encroachment on personal relationships has broader implications for the nature of human connections. The increasing reliance on AI for companionship, social interaction, and even romantic relationships raises questions about the authenticity of these interactions. Technologies like virtual assistants, AI companions, and even sex robots are being marketed as substitutes for human relationships. While these technologies can provide some degree of companionship, they are not capable of offering the genuine emotional intimacy, mutual understanding, and vulnerability that define human relationships.

One of the most significant consequences of AI-driven companionship is the potential for emotional detachment. Relationships are built on a foundation of emotional exchange, vulnerability, and empathy. AI, by contrast, can only simulate these interactions on a superficial level. For instance, virtual assistants or chatbots are programmed to respond to emotions in pre-determined ways based on algorithms, but they do not experience emotions themselves. This creates a situation where individuals may come to rely on AI as a source of comfort, but the relationship remains unidirectional, lacking the reciprocity that is a core component of real human relationships.

In the context of romantic relationships, AI-driven companions might offer the illusion of affection or intimacy, but these interactions are ultimately hollow. Over time, people who replace human relationships with AI companions may find themselves disconnected from the emotional richness that defines genuine romantic bonds. While AI companions may offer an escape from real-world problems or social anxiety, they cannot replace the emotional depth, complexity, and growth that come from interacting with other human beings. This could contribute to a decline in the desire or ability to form authentic, lasting relationships with real people.

Identity Fragmentation: The Psychological Consequences of AI Interaction

Another significant psychological impact of interacting with AI instead of real people is the potential for identity fragmentation. Identity is shaped through social interactions, self-reflection, and engagement with others. When individuals engage with AI, especially those that mimic human behavior, it can create confusion about the nature of their own identity. AI interactions may lack the emotional and contextual depth necessary for people to engage in self-reflection, making it harder for individuals to understand themselves and their place in the world.

For example, when interacting with an AI-driven system that responds in a human-like manner, individuals may begin to internalize these interactions as meaningful social exchanges. Over time, this could affect how individuals view themselves and their relationships with others. They may begin to question what it means to have a "real" relationship and whether AI-driven experiences are sufficient to meet their emotional and psychological needs. This can create a disconnection between one's internal sense of identity and external reality, as individuals may become more focused on the validation provided by AI interactions than the authentic relationships they have with real people.

Furthermore, as AI becomes more personalized and sophisticated, it may blur the line between human and machine interactions. For instance, social media platforms are increasingly using AI to generate content and create personalized experiences for users. This can lead to a situation where individuals are interacting more with algorithms than with actual people. The psychological consequence of this is a diminished sense of agency in personal relationships, as individuals begin to rely more on technology to shape their experiences and decisions. This lack of agency can lead to confusion about personal values, desires, and goals, contributing to a fragmented sense of self.

Balancing AI and Human Connection

As AI continues to evolve and permeate more aspects of daily life, its impact on human identity and relationships is becoming increasingly evident. While AI has the potential to offer convenience and even emotional support, it also poses psychological risks. The shift toward AI-driven interactions can lead to social isolation, loneliness, and emotional detachment, as AI cannot replicate the depth and authenticity of human relationships. Over time, this can contribute to a breakdown in personal identity and a diminished capacity for meaningful social connections.

To mitigate these risks, it is essential to strike a balance between the use of AI and human interaction. AI should not be seen as a replacement for real relationships but as a tool to enhance human experiences. Encouraging more face-to-face interactions, promoting emotional intelligence, and fostering genuine human connections can help counter the potential for loneliness and disconnection caused by AI. As society continues to integrate AI into everyday life, it is crucial to remain mindful of its psychological and social implications, ensuring that technology serves to complement, rather than replace, the fundamental human need for connection.

COUNTERARGUMENTS AND CRITICISMS OF THE DEAD INTERNET THEORY

The "Dead Internet Theory" posits that the internet, once a vibrant and diverse space for human-generated content, is increasingly dominated by artificial intelligence (AI), bots, and commercialized content, resulting in a loss of authenticity and organic interaction. Proponents of this theory argue that much of what users experience online today is no longer shaped by real human engagement but is instead a byproduct of automated systems and corporate control. While this theory has gained traction among some critics of modern internet practices, there are several counterarguments and criticisms that suggest the internet is simply undergoing a natural evolution rather than dying. This essay explores the opposing viewpoints, arguing that the internet is not dead, but rather transforming as new technologies, business models, and user behaviors emerge.

The Internet Is Evolving, Not Dying

One of the primary counterarguments to the Dead Internet Theory is that the internet is not dying, but rather evolving in response to technological advancements and shifting economic models. The internet has always been a dynamic and rapidly changing space. The early days of the internet were characterized by open forums, blogs, and user-generated content, but as technology has advanced, so too have the platforms and business models that dominate the digital landscape. The rise of social media, search engines, and e-commerce platforms has transformed how content is created, shared, and consumed. While these changes may seem drastic or disheartening to those who long for the early days of the internet, they are not signs of decay but rather indicators of growth and adaptation.

For example, social media platforms like Facebook, Twitter, and Instagram have introduced new forms of engagement that allow users to connect, share, and create in ways that were not possible in the 1990s. While it is true that algorithms and AI now play a significant role in curating content on these platforms, they have also facilitated the rise of new forms of expression, from influencers creating personalized content to live streaming, podcasts, and niche online communities. These innovations demonstrate that the internet is evolving to meet the needs of a broader and more diverse user base, rather than signaling its decline.

Moreover, the rise of AI and automation does not necessarily equate to the "death" of the internet. Critics of the Dead Internet Theory argue that AI and bots are tools that, when used properly, can enhance user experience and improve efficiency. For instance, AI-generated content can help automate repetitive tasks, provide more personalized recommendations, and streamline customer service. These technological advancements are improving the way users interact with the digital world, rather than replacing authentic human interaction altogether. Far from signaling the death of the internet, these changes reflect the ongoing evolution of digital platforms, where AI is becoming an integral part of the user experience.

Emerging Business Models and New Technologies

Another major criticism of the Dead Internet Theory is that the commercialization of the internet is not an indication of its death, but rather a necessary evolution to sustain and develop the digital ecosystem. As the internet has grown, so too have the financial and operational demands that come with supporting an increasingly complex and expansive network. Platforms like Google, Facebook, and Amazon have developed business models that rely on advertising, data collection, and content monetization. While these business models have drawn criticism for their influence on content, they are also the means by which the internet remains accessible and functional for billions of users worldwide.

From a business perspective, the use of AI, bots, and algorithms is a logical response to the increasing volume of content and interactions on the internet. With billions of users creating and consuming content daily, it is no longer feasible for human moderators to manage all interactions or for individuals to manually sort through endless amounts of information. AI-driven systems provide scalable solutions that help ensure relevant content reaches the right audience, while also protecting platforms from harmful or inappropriate material. For example, algorithms can help filter spam or malicious content, while bots can provide customer support on a 24/7 basis. This use of AI is a natural extension of the internet's growth and commercial interests, rather than evidence of a decline in human-driven content.

Furthermore, as digital platforms grow, new technologies continue to emerge that offer exciting opportunities for innovation. The advent of decentralized technologies like blockchain, for example, is offering new ways to decentralize content creation and distribution, reducing the control of large corporations over the internet. Web3 technologies promise to create a more open, transparent, and user-controlled internet, where creators and users have more say in how content is shared and monetized. These developments counter the idea that the internet is dying, instead suggesting that the internet is entering a new phase of growth and opportunity, where new models of ownership and engagement are taking shape.

The Persistence of Human Agency

A key criticism of the Dead Internet Theory is that it underestimates the persistence of human agency in shaping the internet. While AI, bots, and algorithms have a growing presence, humans remain at the core of online interactions and content creation. Even with AI-driven systems curating much of the content we see, human creators, businesses, and organizations still produce the vast majority of digital content. The growth of influencer culture, user-generated videos, blogs, and personal social media accounts all demonstrate that individual expression and human-driven content continue to thrive.

Moreover, the internet remains a space where individuals can share their ideas, build communities, and collaborate in ways that were previously impossible. Online forums, independent blogs, and grassroots movements continue to proliferate, showing that while the digital landscape may be increasingly commercialized, there is still room for organic, human-centered interaction. These spaces may not always garner the same level of attention as major social media platforms, but they continue to provide alternatives to algorithm-driven content and demonstrate that human creativity and engagement are far from being replaced.

The internet, far from being dead, is still a vibrant space for human agency and expression. The rise of niche communities, independent content creators, and small businesses reflects the ongoing democratization of the digital world. While it is true that major corporations and AI-driven systems have a significant influence on what we see and engage with online, the idea that human-driven content is vanishing overlooks the many ways in which individuals continue to shape and define the internet.

Critics of the Dead Internet Theory: A Changing Internet Landscape

Critics of the Dead Internet Theory also point out that the internet is not simply becoming more commercialized or automated — it is also diversifying and maturing in response to new needs and challenges. The internet's early days were characterized by a sense of boundless possibility and freedom, but as the digital landscape has grown, it has had to adapt to practical and economic realities. While some may view these changes as signs of decline, they are in fact the internet's response to the complexities of modern life. The internet is a dynamic, ever-evolving ecosystem, and the role of AI and bots is simply part of this transformation.

The development of new technologies, business models, and platforms may indeed create a more centralized digital world, but it also presents new opportunities for growth and innovation. As companies and users explore new ways to connect, share, and create, the internet is evolving in ways that cannot be reduced to a simplistic narrative of decay. From AI-enhanced services to decentralized technologies, the future of the internet remains rich with potential for change and improvement.

Considerations

While the Dead Internet Theory offers a provocative view of the digital world, suggesting that AI, bots, and commercialism have eroded the authenticity of the internet, critics argue that these changes are part of the internet's natural evolution. Far from signaling the death of the internet, the growing influence of AI, algorithms, and commercial interests reflects the ways in which technology is evolving to meet the demands of an increasingly complex and globalized world. The internet is not dead, but rather undergoing a transformation that opens up new possibilities for innovation, user engagement, and content creation. By embracing these changes and exploring new technologies, the digital world will continue to offer opportunities for human creativity, connection, and expression.

COUNTERARGUMENTS AND CRITICISMS OF THE DEAD INTERNET THEORY: AI AND AUTOMATION AS TOOLS, NOT REPLACEMENTS

The "Dead Internet Theory" posits that the internet is rapidly being overtaken by artificial intelligence (AI), bots, and automated systems, leading to the erosion of authentic, human-generated content. Proponents of this theory argue that these forces are gradually replacing human engagement and interaction, making the digital landscape less personal and more artificial. While these concerns highlight legitimate issues about the direction of the internet, a growing body of critics believes that AI and automation should not be viewed as replacements for human interaction, but rather as tools that enhance and support it. This essay will explore how AI and automation can augment human engagement, helping people connect more efficiently, generate meaningful content, and foster new forms of expression and creativity.

AI as a Tool for Enhancing Human Connection

One of the central criticisms of the Dead Internet Theory is its assumption that AI is inherently detrimental to human interaction. While AI is increasingly being integrated into various online platforms, including social media, customer service, and content creation, it is important to consider how these technologies can enhance human experiences rather than diminish them. Instead of replacing genuine human interaction, AI and automation can help to bridge gaps in communication, improve accessibility, and create more personalized experiences that foster deeper connections.

For example, AI-driven chatbots are frequently used in customer service to assist with inquiries and resolve issues more efficiently. Rather than replacing human agents entirely, these systems are designed to handle basic, repetitive tasks, allowing human employees to focus on more complex or emotional customer interactions. This creates a more efficient customer service environment and helps businesses provide 24/7 support. When used properly, AI can enable human employees to engage with customers in more meaningful ways by offloading mundane tasks, allowing for deeper, more personalized interactions when needed.

In addition to enhancing customer service, AI can also facilitate personal connections. For individuals with disabilities, AI technologies can offer innovative solutions for communication. Speech-to-text software and AI-powered voice assistants help people with hearing or speech impairments engage in conversations and access information in new ways. These advancements allow individuals to maintain and enhance social connections that may have been previously hindered by physical limitations. Rather than isolating users or replacing human interaction, AI can serve as an empowering tool that makes communication more inclusive and accessible.

Furthermore, AI technologies can provide individuals with the means to connect with others who share similar interests or experiences, creating virtual communities that foster genuine engagement. For example, recommendation algorithms on platforms like YouTube and Spotify can introduce users to content they may not have discovered on their own, expanding their horizons and creating opportunities for meaningful online interactions. Through personalized content suggestions, AI helps individuals find their communities and engage with others who have similar passions, enhancing rather than diminishing social connection.

AI and Automation as Creative Partners

A key aspect of the Dead Internet Theory is the concern that AI-generated content is eroding human creativity and the authenticity of online interactions. Proponents of the theory argue that AI content, whether in the form of articles, social media posts, or even art, lacks the emotional depth and personal experience that humans bring to their work. However, critics argue that AI can be viewed as a tool that amplifies human creativity rather than replacing it. By automating certain tasks, AI allows creators to focus on more meaningful aspects of their work, pushing the boundaries of what is possible in fields like writing, art, music, and design.

In content creation, AI can assist writers and artists by generating ideas, drafting preliminary outlines, or even providing inspiration. For instance, AI tools like OpenAI's GPT-3 can help writers develop narratives, suggest vocabulary, or create content in a matter of seconds. This technology does not replace the writer but rather serves as a partner that aids in overcoming writer's block and enhancing productivity. Many writers use AI to quickly generate drafts or brainstorm ideas, which they can then refine and personalize, incorporating their own experiences, emotions, and creative flair into the final product. This collaborative approach between humans and machines allows for more efficient content creation while maintaining the authenticity of the individual creator's voice.

Similarly, in the realm of art, AI tools like DeepArt and DALL·E are being used by artists to experiment with new styles, generate visual concepts, and explore novel ideas. These tools help artists push the boundaries of their creativity by offering new perspectives and possibilities. However, the final work remains a product of human ingenuity and imagination. AI in this context serves as a tool that enhances the artistic process rather than replacing the artist's unique input. As technology continues to evolve, artists can leverage AI to create more complex and sophisticated works, leading to a greater diversity of artistic expression in the digital age.

Moreover, AI's ability to automate certain tasks does not necessarily mean that human-generated content is in decline. On the contrary, automation can increase the overall amount of content created, freeing up time for humans to focus on higher-level creative endeavors. For example, automated content generation in areas such as journalism can speed up the production of routine news articles, leaving human journalists more time to investigate stories, write in-depth reports, and engage in long-form content creation. By handling repetitive or data-heavy tasks, AI allows journalists to focus on the critical aspects of storytelling, improving the quality of the content while increasing efficiency.

AI as a Facilitator of New Forms of Expression

AI's role in the creative process is not limited to traditional content creation. As AI technology advances, it is opening up entirely new forms of expression and interaction that were previously impossible. For instance, AI-powered platforms have enabled the development of interactive digital experiences, such as virtual reality (VR) worlds and augmented reality (AR) applications, where users can engage in dynamic and immersive environments. These technologies allow people to explore new realities, create their own digital avatars, and interact with others in ways that are not constrained by physical limitations.

Moreover, AI has enabled the rise of new genres of music, such as generative music, where AI algorithms create compositions based on user inputs or pre-programmed patterns. Musicians and producers can use these AI-generated compositions as starting points, combining them with their own ideas to create innovative new sounds. In this way, AI is not replacing the musician but expanding the possibilities of musical expression, allowing for more experimentation and collaboration between humans and machines.

These advancements highlight the evolving nature of the internet and the ways in which AI is transforming creative industries. Far from signaling the decline of human-generated content, AI is offering new opportunities for self-expression, creativity, and engagement that were previously unimaginable. The fusion of human ingenuity with machine intelligence is creating an exciting future where the possibilities for new forms of art, entertainment, and connection are endless.

The Importance of Human Agency

While AI is undoubtedly a powerful tool, critics of the Dead Internet Theory also argue that human agency remains a crucial factor in shaping the future of the internet. Humans are the architects of AI technologies, and as such, they retain the power to determine how these tools are used and to ensure that they serve the collective good. Rather than seeing AI as a force that threatens to overshadow human voices, critics contend that it is up to society to ensure that AI enhances rather than replaces human interactions and creativity.

One of the main benefits of AI is its ability to handle large-scale data processing and automation, which allows humans to focus on higher-level decision-making, creativity, and emotional engagement. The relationship between humans and AI is not inherently one of replacement, but rather one of collaboration. As technology continues to advance, it is crucial for individuals, businesses, and governments to maintain oversight over how AI is integrated into society. By implementing ethical guidelines and prioritizing human-driven values, AI can become a tool that supports, rather than undermines, human engagement and expression.

Considerations

In response to the concerns raised by the Dead Internet Theory, it is clear that AI and automation should not be viewed as forces that replace human interaction or content, but as tools that can enhance and support them. By streamlining repetitive tasks, enabling creative collaboration, and opening new avenues for self-expression, AI has the potential to improve the digital experience and empower individuals to create more meaningful content. Far from signaling the decline of human agency, these technologies offer new opportunities for connection, creativity, and innovation. As long as human agency remains central to the development and application of AI, the future of the internet can be one where humans and machines work together to build a more connected, creative, and vibrant digital world.

COUNTERARGUMENTS AND CRITICISMS OF THE DEAD INTERNET THEORY: EVIDENCE OF REAL, HUMAN-CENTERED CONTENT

The "Dead Internet Theory" posits that the internet, once a vibrant space for human-centered content, is increasingly being dominated by artificial intelligence (AI), bots, and automated systems. According to proponents of the theory, this shift is leading to the loss of authenticity in online interactions, as human-generated content is being overshadowed by machine-generated material. While the growth of automation and AI has undoubtedly changed the digital landscape, critics of the Dead Internet Theory argue that it overlooks the ongoing existence of real, human-centered content. Despite the rise of bots, algorithms, and commercial interests, there are still vast spaces on the internet where genuine human interaction thrives. Niche communities, independent media, and activist movements continue to provide platforms for authentic voices and meaningful exchanges. This essay explores how these spaces offer compelling evidence that the internet is not dying but evolving in ways that still allow for human agency and expression.

Niche Communities: The Persistence of Human-Centered Interaction

One of the most significant counterarguments to the Dead Internet Theory is the continued existence of niche communities where human-centered content flourishes. While mainstream platforms like Facebook, Twitter, and Instagram may be increasingly dominated by algorithmic content and AI-driven recommendations, smaller, independent forums and online spaces remain fertile ground for genuine human interaction. These niche communities often focus on specific interests or shared experiences, allowing users to engage in deep, authentic discussions that are less influenced by commercial pressures or algorithmic manipulation.

Platforms such as Reddit, Discord, and smaller online forums host communities where people come together to discuss hobbies, share personal stories, and offer support. For example, Reddit has thousands of subreddits dedicated to everything from obscure television shows to specific health conditions. These subreddits foster direct human interaction, where users share real experiences, ask questions, and offer advice. Unlike the algorithm-driven content on mainstream social media platforms, the interactions within these communities are shaped by shared passions and interests rather than by paid advertisements or AI-generated content. Even though automated systems are used to moderate content, these communities are still primarily human-driven, with users shaping the tone, nature, and substance of the conversations.

In addition, platforms like Discord provide a space for real-time communication among people with common interests, where text chats, voice chats, and video calls facilitate genuine, human connections. These communities, while supported by technology, are far from artificial. They are grounded in authentic human relationships and interactions. The ongoing vibrancy of these niche spaces demonstrates that the internet is far from being overtaken by bots or AI; instead, it continues to offer rich environments for people to connect and collaborate in meaningful ways.

Independent Media: A Haven for Human-Centered Content

Another key criticism of the Dead Internet Theory is the ongoing presence of independent media outlets that offer authentic, human-generated content. While mainstream media has increasingly relied on automated systems to generate news articles, advertisements, and even opinion pieces, independent media outlets have flourished in the age of the internet, providing a platform for voices that might not otherwise be heard in the traditional media landscape.

Independent journalism and alternative news outlets often focus on in-depth reporting, investigative journalism, and human interest stories that are shaped by real-world experiences and reporting. Websites like The Intercept, ProPublica, and various independent bloggers continue to produce high-quality, human-centered content that resists the commercialization and automation seen in mainstream media. These outlets rely on human reporters, editors, and writers who engage with real-world issues and produce content that reflects genuine experiences and perspectives.

Moreover, with the rise of platforms like Substack, Medium, and Patreon, many independent journalists and content creators have found ways to monetize their work while maintaining editorial independence. These platforms allow creators to bypass traditional advertising-driven business models, allowing for more human-centered content that reflects the authentic voices of creators rather than the interests of corporate advertisers or AI algorithms. The growth of these platforms demonstrates that while automation and commercial pressures shape parts of the internet, there are still significant spaces where human creativity and engagement are at the forefront.

Additionally, platforms like YouTube and podcasts have allowed individuals to share their personal stories, expert knowledge, and unique perspectives with a global audience. While these platforms use algorithms to recommend content, they also allow creators to build independent, niche followings based on genuine human engagement. The internet remains a powerful tool for storytelling, where content is still produced by people with real experiences and ideas to share.

Activist Movements: The Role of Human Agency in Social Change

Activist movements represent another compelling example of human-centered content thriving on the internet, even in the age of automation. From social justice causes to environmental activism, the internet remains a vital tool for organizing, raising awareness, and mobilizing people around important issues. While bots and AI may play a role in shaping narratives, the core of these movements remains driven by passionate individuals who are motivated by shared goals and values.

Social media platforms like Twitter and Instagram have been instrumental in amplifying social justice movements, such as Black Lives Matter, #MeToo, and environmental campaigns like Fridays for Future. These movements rely on real people to share their stories, organize protests, and engage in activism, creating genuine, human-centered content that challenges the status quo and sparks societal change. Despite the commercialization of these platforms, they remain central to the dissemination of human-generated messages that resonate with people around the world.

In addition, decentralized platforms and encrypted messaging services like Telegram and Signal provide spaces for activists to communicate and organize without the interference of corporate interests or automated systems. These tools allow individuals to protect their privacy while engaging in activism and social change, highlighting the importance of human agency in shaping the digital world. While bots and AI may be used by certain parties to manipulate or suppress activism, the enduring success of grassroots movements demonstrates that human voices and experiences continue to drive significant social change online.

The Internet as a Space for Diversity of Thought

Despite the rise of algorithmic content and the dominance of major tech companies, the internet remains a diverse space where different ideas, cultures, and perspectives can thrive. The ability to express dissent, critique authority, and engage in dialogue with others is still very much a part of the online experience, particularly in independent media and niche communities.

Critics of the Dead Internet Theory argue that the rise of AI and bots does not necessarily result in a uniform or homogenized digital ecosystem. In fact, the internet continues to provide opportunities for individuals to find and engage with content that aligns with their personal values, interests, and experiences. By participating in niche communities, following independent creators, and engaging in activism, users can access a wide array of authentic, human-centered content that is tailored to their unique needs and desires.

Moreover, the internet's decentralized nature allows for the creation of alternative spaces where people can engage in more meaningful, less commercialized exchanges. While social media platforms and search engines may prioritize AI-generated content or algorithmic recommendations, there are still countless independent websites, forums, and blogs where individuals share their thoughts, express their creativity, and participate in discussions that are not influenced by commercial interests or automation.

Considerations

In conclusion, the Dead Internet Theory's claim that the internet is being overtaken by bots, AI, and automation to the point of losing human authenticity is challenged by the ongoing presence of real, human-centered content across the digital landscape. Niche communities, independent media, and activist movements continue to thrive, offering spaces for individuals to engage with one another, share their experiences, and create content that is deeply personal and human-driven. While the internet has certainly evolved, and automation plays a significant role in shaping the digital environment, these spaces demonstrate that the internet remains a dynamic platform for genuine human interaction, creativity, and social change. Rather than signaling the death of human-generated content, the persistence of these human-centered spaces underscores the resilience of authenticity in the digital age. The internet, while evolving, continues to be a space where real people can connect, create, and inspire each other.

FINAL CONSIDERATIONS

The Dead Internet Theory suggests that the internet, once a vibrant space for authentic human interaction and content creation, is increasingly being overtaken by artificial intelligence (AI), bots, and algorithm-driven content. Supporters of this theory argue that these automated systems are flooding the digital landscape with non-human material, resulting in a significant decline in genuine human engagement.

One of the main points supporting the theory is the growing presence of bots on social media platforms, such as Twitter and Instagram. These bots create fake accounts, generate automated posts, and amplify certain narratives, often making it difficult for users to discern real content from machine-generated material. In addition, the increasing reliance on AI for content creation, such as AI-written articles, social media posts, and even deepfake videos, contributes to the proliferation of artificial content that mimics human writing and interaction but lacks authenticity.

The rise of algorithm-driven platforms also plays a key role in the Dead Internet Theory. Social media platforms, news websites, and search engines use algorithms to prioritize content that generates the most engagement, often favoring AI-generated or commercially-driven content over organic human voices. This trend leads to a more uniform, commercialized digital ecosystem, where genuine human expression is drowned out by algorithmically optimized material. Together, these factors contribute to the belief that the internet is losing its original, human-centered nature, becoming dominated by automation and artificial content.

The future of the internet is a subject of intense speculation, especially as artificial intelligence (AI) and automation continue to shape its evolution. As AI tools become more advanced, it is likely that machine-generated content will become an even greater presence online. From news articles and social media posts to customer service interactions and deepfake videos, AI is poised to further dominate content creation, often driven by algorithms designed to maximize engagement. This could lead to a digital landscape where automated systems produce a significant portion of the material users encounter, raising concerns about the erosion of authenticity and the human touch.

However, there is potential for human interaction to reclaim its space on the internet. While commercial pressures and the growth of AI-driven content are undeniable, human-centered digital spaces continue to thrive. Niche communities, independent creators, and social movements still foster authentic engagement. The rise of decentralized platforms, user-driven content, and movements advocating for digital rights and privacy suggest that the internet may evolve in a way that allows for more organic, human-driven interaction. With growing awareness of privacy concerns and the need for more authentic online experiences, users and creators may push back against over-reliance on AI and algorithmic control.

The future of the internet may therefore see a balance between AI's role in enhancing user experiences—through personalized recommendations and content generation—and the reclamation of human agency, where individuals can carve out spaces for genuine interaction, creativity, and discourse. As technology evolves, it will be crucial for users, creators, and policymakers to navigate this balance, ensuring that the internet remains a platform for both innovation and authentic human connection.

The Potential Dangers of Losing Organic Human Interactions Online

The internet has undeniably transformed the way we communicate, learn, and connect. What began as a vast network of human-centered interactions, where individuals shared personal stories, ideas, and experiences, has gradually evolved into a digital space increasingly dominated by artificial intelligence (AI), bots, and algorithm-driven content. The rise of automated systems and the commercialization of online platforms have significantly altered the way we interact online. As human engagement becomes overshadowed by machine-generated material, there are growing concerns about the potential dangers of losing genuine, organic interactions on the internet. This essay aims to call for awareness about this shift, urging readers to critically examine the content they encounter and support platforms that prioritize human-centered experiences.

The Erosion of Authentic Human Interaction

The internet, once a platform for diverse, organic content, has become increasingly dominated by AI-generated material and algorithmic content. Automated bots flood social media with fake accounts, posts, and comments, manipulating conversations and distorting the authenticity of online interactions. This phenomenon not only clouds the distinction between real and artificial content but also creates an environment where human voices can be drowned out by algorithms and machine-generated noise. News articles, social media posts, and even video content are now often produced by AI, designed to mimic human language and behavior but lacking the depth, nuance, and emotional authenticity that define human interaction.

One of the most concerning aspects of this shift is the decline of genuine human connections. The internet was once a space where people from around the world could share their ideas, build relationships, and exchange diverse viewpoints. However, as AI-driven content takes over, it can be difficult to discern whether the posts and interactions we encounter are from real people or automated systems. This not only stifles authentic communication but also leads to a homogenization of ideas, as algorithms prioritize content that generates clicks and engagement rather than content that fosters meaningful dialogue. In such an environment, users may find themselves engaging less with one another and more with an endless stream of machine-generated content designed to capture their attention.

The Psychological and Social Implications

The rise of algorithm-driven content and AI-generated material has psychological and social implications for internet users. With the increasing dominance of non-human content, individuals may experience feelings of isolation, mistrust, and disconnection. Social media, once a space for personal expression and human connection, has become a platform where commercial interests, algorithms, and bots often dictate what we see and engage with. As a result, users may find themselves interacting less with real people and more with artificial entities or content that lacks emotional depth.

Additionally, the spread of misinformation and fake news is amplified in a digital environment dominated by AI-generated material. Bots and automated systems can create convincing but false narratives, shaping public opinion and spreading disinformation at a rapid pace. The lack of human oversight and accountability in such systems can lead to a breakdown of trust in online content, further contributing to a sense of uncertainty and alienation.

The psychological toll of these changes can be profound. People may begin to question the authenticity of the interactions they have online, leading to a sense of disillusionment with the digital world. If the internet continues to prioritize AI-driven content over human voices, it risks creating a digital landscape where people feel disconnected from one another and less inclined to engage in meaningful online exchanges.

Critical Examination of Content

In light of these concerns, it is essential for internet users to critically examine the content they encounter. We must recognize that not all content on the internet is created equally, and much of it is now shaped by algorithms, paid advertisements, or AI systems. These systems prioritize engagement and profit, often at the expense of authenticity and depth. By being mindful of the content we consume, we can make more informed choices about the platforms we use and the information we trust.

This critical awareness begins with questioning the sources of the content we encounter. Are we engaging with content that is written, shared, or created by real people, or is it being driven by AI or automated systems? Are the voices we hear diverse and representative, or are we only encountering content designed to maximize clicks and engagement? By being more discerning, we can help push back against the dominance of machine-generated material and support platforms that prioritize human-centered content.

Supporting Human-Centered Platforms

To counter the rise of AI-driven content and bots, it is vital to support platforms that prioritize human engagement and authenticity. There are still spaces on the internet where genuine human interaction flourishes, including independent media outlets, niche communities, and grassroots movements. These platforms offer opportunities for people to share their experiences, exchange ideas, and engage with one another in meaningful ways, without the interference of bots or commercial interests.

By supporting independent creators, subscribing to human-centered news outlets, and participating in online communities that foster authentic dialogue, we can help ensure that the internet remains a platform for genuine human connection. These spaces allow for more diverse perspectives and provide a counterbalance to the homogenized, commercialized content that dominates much of the digital landscape today.

In addition, advocating for better digital literacy and privacy protections can empower users to make more informed decisions about their online activities. As we continue to navigate an increasingly automated digital world, it is crucial to prioritize platforms that uphold ethical standards and allow for free, authentic expression.

Conclusions

The internet's shift from a vibrant space of organic human interactions to one dominated by AI, bots, and algorithm-driven content represents a significant concern for the future of online communication. The loss of authentic human engagement could have far-reaching psychological and social implications, including feelings of isolation, mistrust, and disconnection. However, it is not too late to reclaim the internet as a space for genuine, human-centered interactions. By critically examining the content we encounter and supporting platforms that prioritize authentic engagement, we can help ensure that the digital world remains a space for meaningful connection, diversity of thought, and human creativity. Now more than ever, it is crucial for internet users to remain vigilant and proactive in preserving the human element of the internet, fostering an online ecosystem where real voices continue to be heard.

3 hours.

28 prompts.

152 pages.